A Colour Atlas of Physical Signs
in Cardiovascular Disease

-7. JUN. 1989   30/ MAY 1993

-6. AUG. 1989   22. JUL 03

12. OCT. 1989   13. SEP. 1993
-7. JUL. 1994

21. MAR 95   16. JUL 14

-4. JAN. 1989   13. AUG 97

29. FEB. 1990   13. APR 99

-9. MAY 1990   13. MAY 99
10. JUN 99

28. JUL 1990   20. NOV 00

PLEASE ENTER ON LOAN SLIP:

AUTHOR: SHAPIRO, L.M.

TITLE:
COLOUR ATLAS OF PHYSICAL SIGNS
IN CARDIOVASCULAR DISEASE

ACCESSION NO:	CLASS MARK:
SA 881029	WG 141

A Colour Atlas of

PHYSICAL SIGNS IN CARDIOVASCULAR DISEASE

Leonard M. Shapiro
MD, MRCP
Consultant Cardiologist
Papworth and Addenbrookes Hospitals, Cambridge

Kim M. Fox
MD, FRCP
Consultant Cardiologist
National Heart Hospital, London

Wolfe Medical Publications Ltd

Copyright © L. M. Shapiro, K. M. Fox, 1989
First published 1989 by Wolfe Medical Publications Ltd
Printed by W. S. Cowell Ltd, Ipswich, England
ISBN 0 7234 0993 5 (Cased)
ISBN 0 7234 1573 0 (Limp)

A CIP catalogue record for this book is available from the British Library.

This book is one of the titles in the series of Wolfe Medical Atlases, a series
that brings together the world's largest systematic published collection of
diagnostic colour photographs.

For a full list of Atlases in the series, plus forthcoming titles and details of
our surgical, dental and veterinary Atlases, please write to Wolfe Medical
Publications Ltd, 2-16 Torrington Place, London WC1E 7LT, England.

CONTENTS

ACKNOWLEDGEMENTS

We are indebted to the many colleagues who have contributed illustrations for this text. In particular we would like to acknowledge the help of Mr G. Castle without whose help the phonocardiograms would not have been possible. We would also like to acknowledge Mr B. Richards who provided invaluable help with the photography of the figures. We wish to acknowledge the departments of medical photography where we have previously worked including Dudley Road Hospital, Hammersmith Hospital, Brompton Hospital and Wythenshawe Hospital. We wish to thank the following who have lent us many illustrations: Dr P. Crean, Dr E. Olsen, Dr Carole Warnes, Professor R. Anderson, Dr John Davies, Dr Alison P. Howat, Dr D. Longmore, Dr J. Gibbs, Dr D. Thompson, Dr D. Underwood and Miss Caroline Westgate. Most of the patients illustrated in the text were under the care of the physicians at the National Heart Hospital without whose support this text would not have been possible. The help of Miss Kathy Back in typing the text is gratefully acknowledged.

PREFACE

Examination of the cardiovascular system is a cornerstone in the clinical examination of the patient. Although many new techniques are now available for the investigation of patients with heart disease, they should be considered as a supplement to a careful clinical examination. In this atlas we have approached the clinical examination in the classical manner starting with the general appearance and then proceeding to the more detailed examination of the cardiovascular system. As often as possible, we have tried to illustrate the important clinical features with the underlying pathology. This is not intended to be a text of cardiac pathology, but the pathology is simply to act as an aide-mémoire.

This book is aimed at a wide audience. Hopefully it will be of value to physicians and general practitioners as well as to medical students and doctors studying for further qualifications. It is impossible to illustrate every clinical manifestation and every subtle variation, but an attempt has been made to illustrate all the important conditions and some of the rarer ones.

1. CLINICAL EXAMINATION OF THE PATIENT

The clinical features of heart disease are not confined to the cardiovascular system and it is essential that a full general medical examination is undertaken. This must include a general overview of the patient with examination of the mouth, hands, face, eyes, feet and legs and finally the retina. Evidence of associated conditions that may lead to heart disease such as inherited disorders, endocrine conditions, anaemia and connective tissue diseases must be sought. In addition, the complications of heart disease may also be in evidence, in particular heart failure, cyanosis, jaundice, endocarditis and signs of vascular occlusion.

GENERAL APPEARANCE

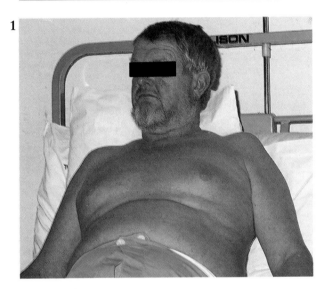

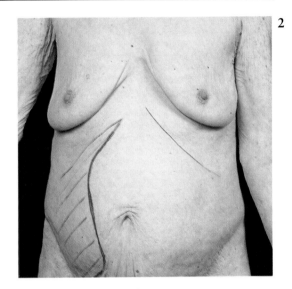

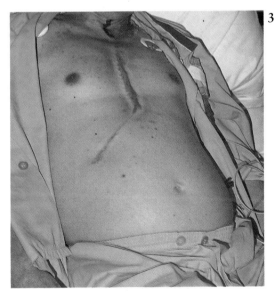

1–3 Patients with left ventricular failure will tend to sit upright in bed (**1**). The development of congestive heart failure results in hepatomegaly (**2**) and ascites (**3**).

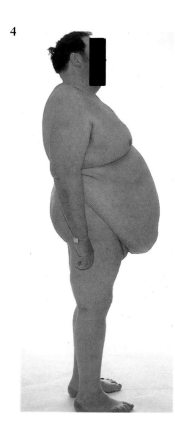

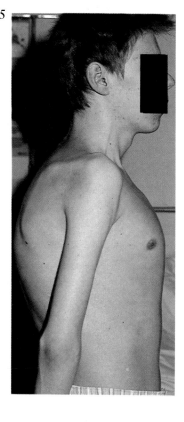

4 Gross obesity is associated with an increased incidence of coronary disease and may also lead to cor pulmonale by restricting ventilation.

5 Barrel chest deformity may occur secondary to long-standing heart disease, particularly in children and adolescents.

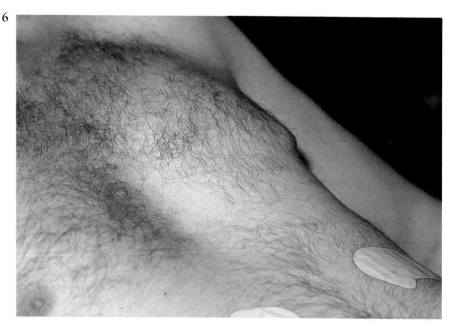

6 Pigeon chest deformities are commonly associated with heart disease and can lead to murmurs in a patient with a normal heart.

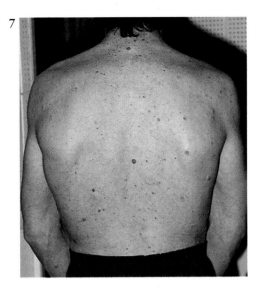

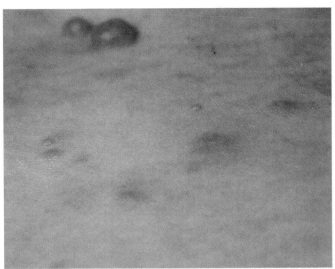

7 & 8 Patients with von Recklinghausen's disease may have phaeochromocytoma causing hypertension or cardiac tumour. Typically von Recklinghausen's disease causes a scoliosis (7) and the classical features of neurofibroma (8) and café-au-lait spots. Lenticulosis may have similar skin lesions, but is extremely rare and is associated with hypertrophic cardiomyopathy.

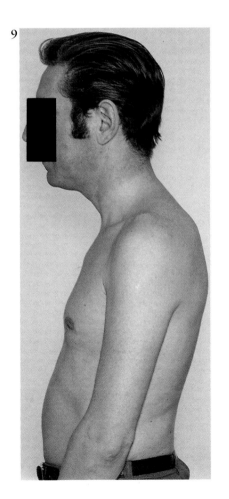

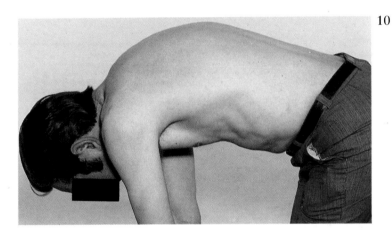

9 & 10 Ankylosing spondylitis associated with aortic regurgitation causes loss of a normal spinal curvature (9) with limited flexion (10).

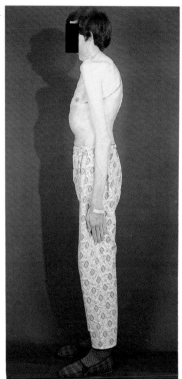

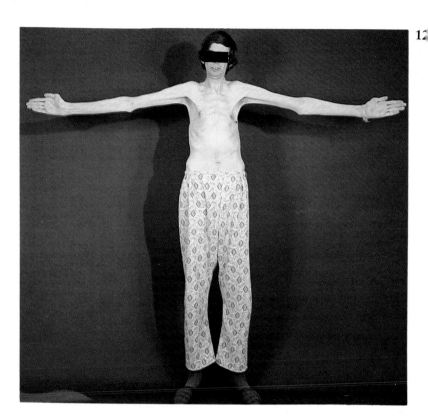

11–13 The skeletal manifestations of Marfan's syndrome are frequently associated with heart disease, particularly diseases of the valve and root. These include excessive height and arachnodactyly (**11, 12**). Homocystinuria may have similar skeletal and cardiac manifestations, though the patients have fair hair (**13**).

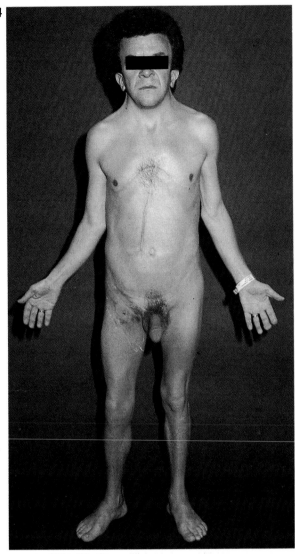

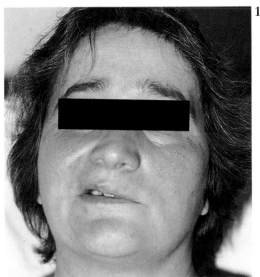

15 In patients presenting with cerebrovascular accidents, a cardiac source of embolus should always be sought. Common causes include atrial fibrillation, mitral valve disease and endocarditis.

14 Noonan's syndrome, which is associated with pulmonary stenosis, atrial septal defect and hypertrophic cardiomyopathy, has classical clinical features of male Turner's syndrome, i.e. neck webbing, wide carrying angles, short stature and hypogonadism.

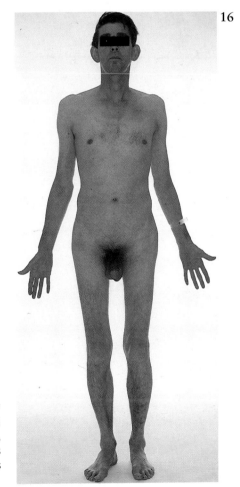

16 A variety of muscular dystrophies may lead to heart-muscle disease and present with heart failure. These include Duchenne's, myotonia dystrophica and Friedreich's ataxia. The widespread muscle wasting is clearly evident in this example.

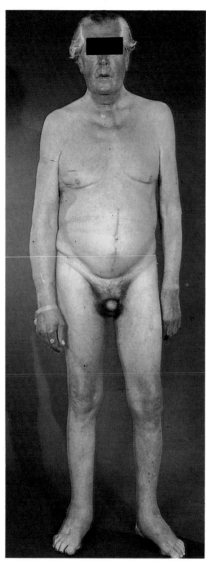

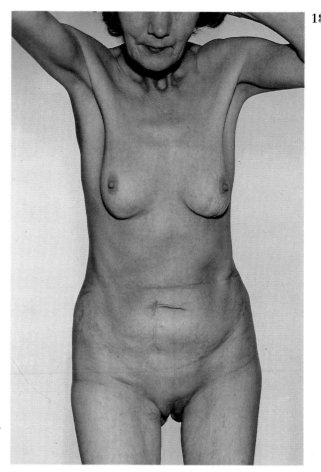

18 Hypopituitarism may lead to postural hypotension; the typical features of hypopituitarism include loss of body hair.

17 Carcinoid syndrome is a rare cause of tricuspid and pulmonary valve disease. Typical features include flushing, dermatographia and hepatomegaly.

19 Cushing's syndrome is a rare cause of hypertension. Characteristically, abdominal striae may occur; this was due to steroid ingestion.

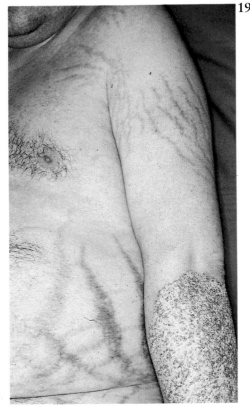

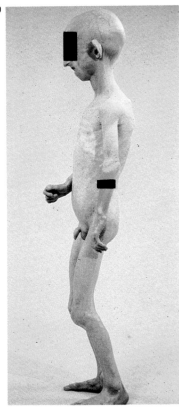

20 Progeria, an extremely rare disease of premature ageing, often presents with cardiac disease.

21 Following correction of congenital heart lesions, obstruction of the inferior vena cava may occur causing dilatation of the veins over the trunk.

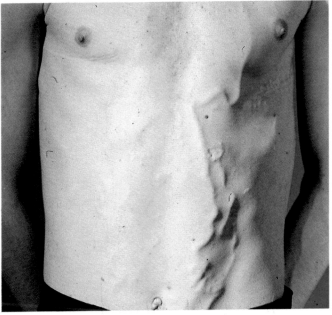

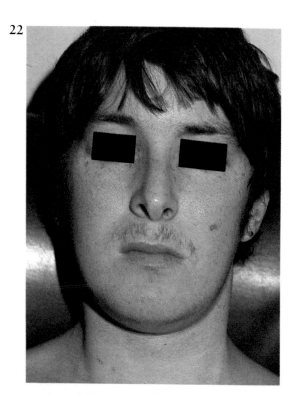

22 Jaundice is an important secondary manifestation of cardiac disease. It may occur in congestive heart failure due to hepatic congestion, in haemolytic anaemia secondary to prosthetic valve insertion and in other conditions such as endocarditis.

23 & 24 A malar flush may occur in mitral valve disease or where the cardiac output is low. The severity of the malar flush (mild **23**, severe **24**) is unrelated to the severity of the underlying heart condition.

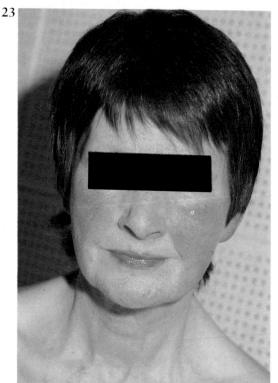

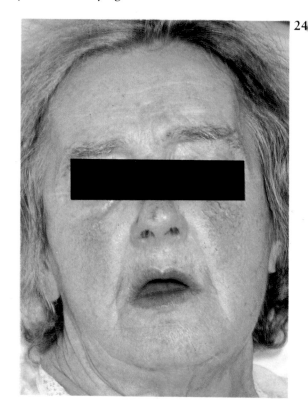

25 & 26 Myxoedema can be recognised by a typical facies, with thickening and puffiness of the skin of the face and eyes (**25**); the hair may be brittle (**26**) and sparse. Myxoedema is associated with a bradycardia, heart failure, pericardial effusion and premature coronary disease due to hyperlipidaemia.

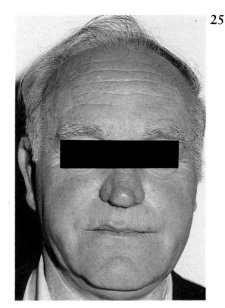

25

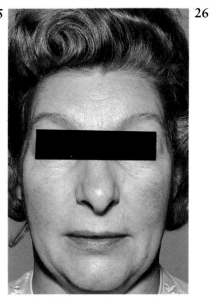

26

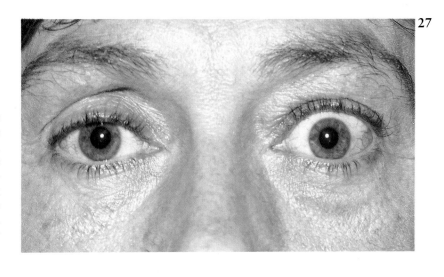

27

27–29 Hyperthyroidism is associated with tachycardias and high output heart failure. Classical physical signs include exophthalmus, lid lag and retraction (**27**). Although most commonly the thyroid is diffusely enlarged, occasionally a thyroid nodule (**28, 29**) may be present.

28

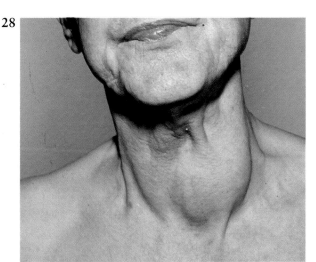

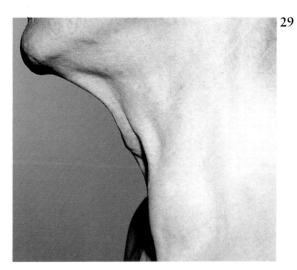

29

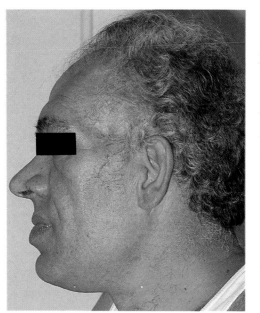
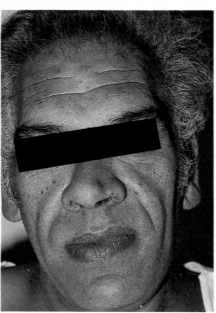

30 & 31 Acromegaly is associated with hypertension, premature coronary disease and rarely heart-muscle disease. The facial appearances of acromegaly include overgrowth of the supra-orbital ridge with forward displacement of the zygoma (**30**) and expansion of the frontal sinuses (**31**). Growth of the mandible leads to prognathism.

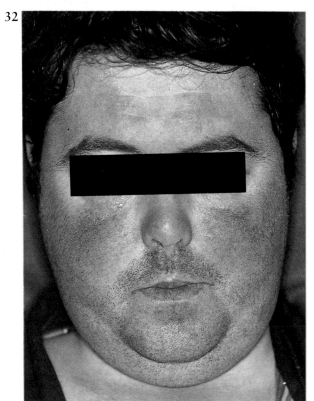
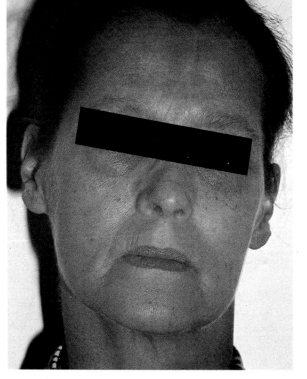

32 Cushing's syndrome is a rare cause of hypertension. The typical moon face is clearly evident.

33 Addison's disease is a very rare cause of postural hypotension. There is exaggerated pigmentation.

34 & 35 Williams' syndrome (hypercalcaemia of infancy), which has a typical elfin-like facies with low set ears, is commonly associated with supravalvular aortic stenosis, coarctation of the aorta and peripheral pulmonary artery stenosis.

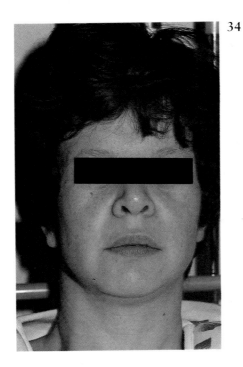

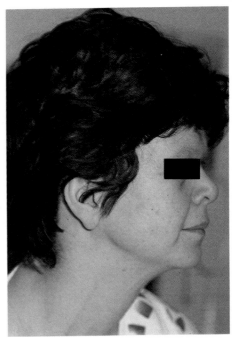

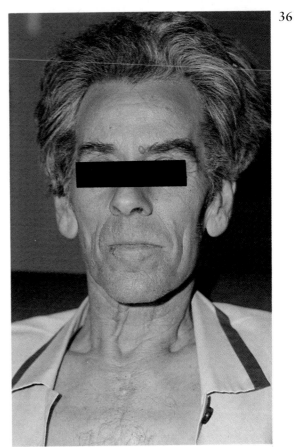

36 Haemochromatosis and Wilson's disease are rare causes of cardiomyopathy. Haemochromatosis may be recognised by the slate grey pigmentation of the skin due to iron deposition. Wilson's disease causes a similar pigmentation due to abnormal copper deposition.

 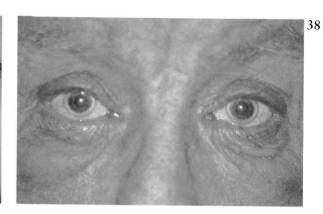

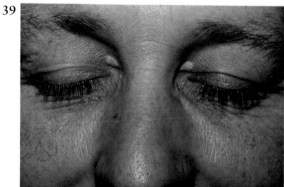 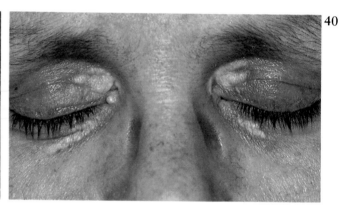

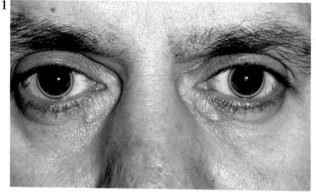

37–41 Clinical evidence of hyperlipidaemia should be sought in any young patient presenting with angina pectoris. The presence of an arcus juvenilis in a young patient (37) is a strong indicator of hyperlipidaemia and coronary disease. In contrast, the presence of arcus senilis does not carry similar risks in the elderly (38). Facial xanthelasma is an important finding in hyperlipidaemia; this may be nodular (39) or planar (40). Occasionally an arcus and xanthelasma may be present in the same patient with hyperlipidaemia (41).

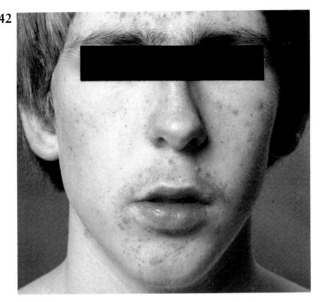 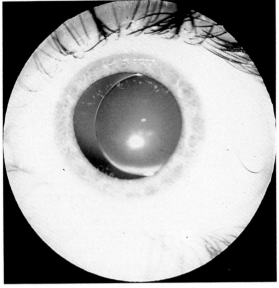

42 & 43 Marfan's syndrome is a defect in collagen metabolism leading to disease of the aorta, aortic valve and the mitral valve ring; the face is long and narrow (**42**) and characteristically the lens is posteriorly dislocated (**43**).

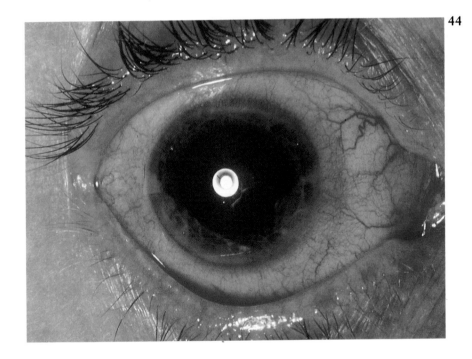

44 Ankylosing spondylitis associated with aortic root disease may manifest itself as an iritis. Ankylosing spondylitis may also lead to complete heart block due to disease of the conducting system.

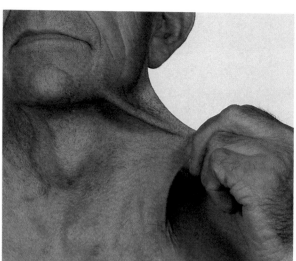 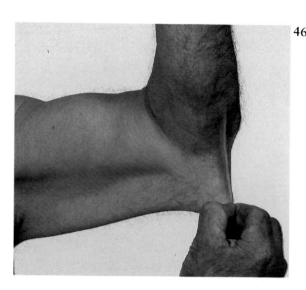

45 & 46 Diseases of connective tissue such as Ehlers–Danlos syndrome (**45**) and pseudoxanthoma elasticum (**46**) are associated with aortic root disease causing dissecting aneurysm and aneurysm of the sinus of Valsalva. Ehlers–Danlos syndrome is evident clinically by the presence of loose inelastic skin. Pseudoxanthoma elasticum has similar clinical features with angioid streaks in the retina and may present with coronary arterial thrombi causing acute myocardial infarction.

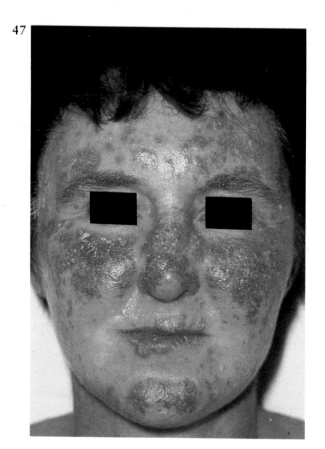 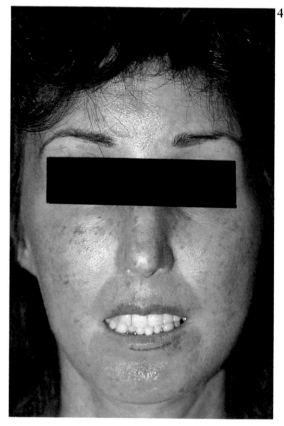

47 & 48 Connective tissue disorders may be associated with pulmonary hypertension, pericarditis and fibrous replacement of the myocardium. Systemic lupus erythematosus (**47**) is characterised by a butterfly rash whilst the typical appearance of scleroderma (**48**) is oedema and tight skin with contraction around the mouth.

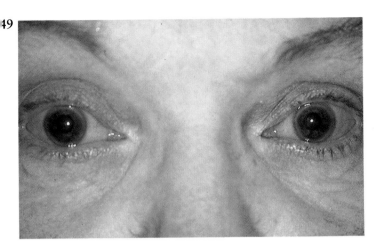

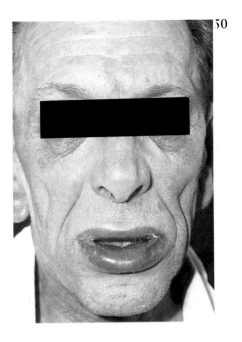

49 Osteogenesis imperfecta is an inherited disorder of collagen metabolism and in milder forms, patients survive to adulthood. The bony abnormalities predominate, but cardiovascular manifestations include diseases of the aortic root leading to aortic dissection. Characteristically these patients have blue sclera.

50 Rarely, acute hypertension may lead to heart failure as in this example of acute glomerulonephritis causing facial oedema.

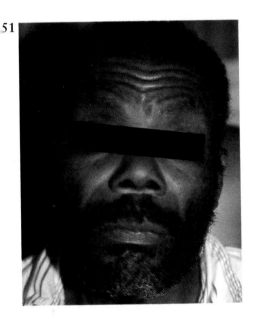

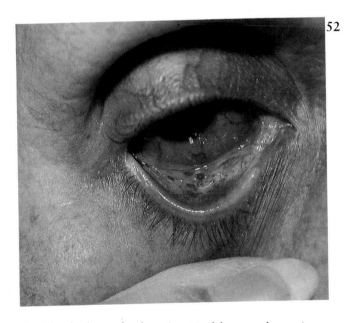

51 Cardiovascular syphilis, though rare, should always be considered in patients presenting with diseases of the ascending aorta such as aortic regurgitation or coronary ostial stenosis leading to angina or acute myocardial infarction. The typical facial features include a staring appearance with loss of facial expression.

52 The finding of subconjunctival haemorrhages is a pathognomonic feature of infective endocarditis.

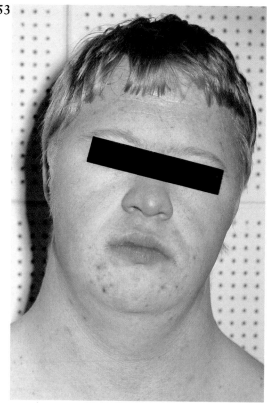

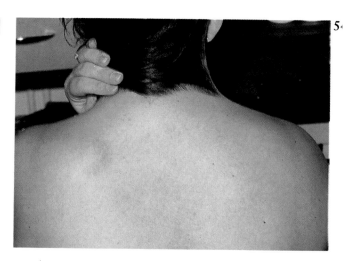

53–55 Congenital chromosomal abnormalities often lead to serious congenital heart disease. Down's syndrome or trisomy 21 (53) is characteristically associated with Fallot's tetralogy, pulmonary stenosis and atrioventricular septal defect; in Turner's syndrome (XO) there is typically webbing of the neck with a low set hairline and associated coarctation of the aorta and bicuspid aortic valves (54). Noonan's syndrome or male Turner's syndrome has a similar facial appearance to Turner's with hypertelorism and neck webbing and may be associated with pulmonary stenosis, hypertrophic cardiomyopathy or atrial septal defect (55).

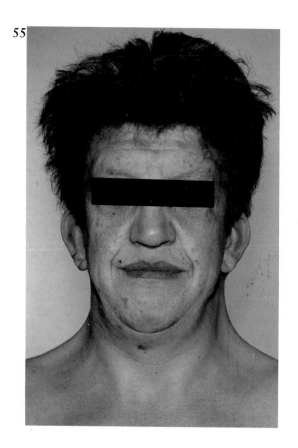

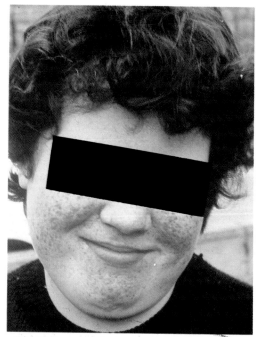

56 Tuberous sclerosis has the facial appearance of adenoma sebaceum; the heart is involved by intramural rhabdomyomata and pedunculated tumours.

THE MOUTH

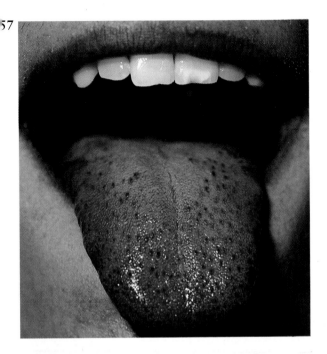

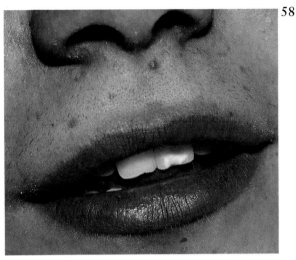

57 & 58 Central cyanosis is most easily seen around the tongue (57) and lips (58).

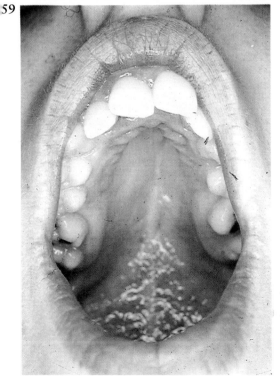

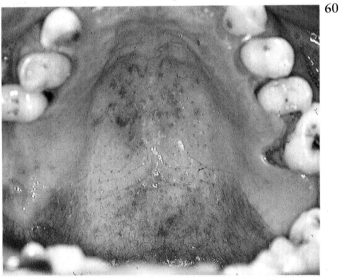

60 Palatal petechiae, a feature of infective endocarditis, are an immunological phenomenon similar to conjunctival and splinter haemorrhages.

59 A high arched and narrow palate is a characteristic feature of Marfan's syndrome.

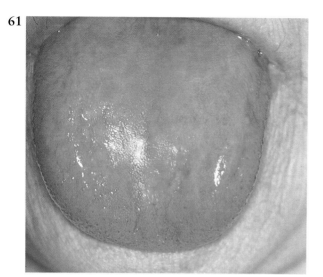

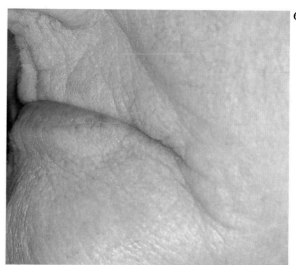

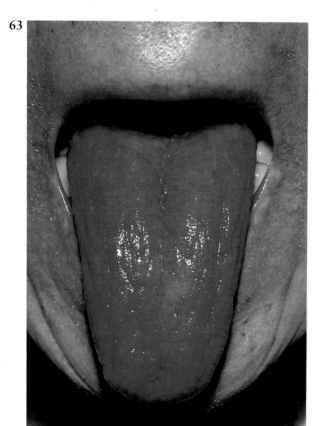

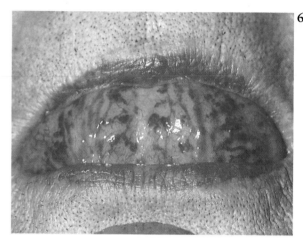

61–64 Features of anaemia may be evident on examination of the mouth. A smooth tongue (**61**) and angular cheilitis (**62**) occur in iron deficiency anaemia. A beefy tongue is present in patients with pernicious anaemia (**63**); patients with hereditary haemorrhagic telangiectasia have vascular abnormalities around the mouth and under the tongue (**64**) and develop chronic blood loss into the gut causing an iron deficiency anaemia. Anaemias are important in cardiovascular disease as they may exacerbate underlying conditions such as coronary artery disease and heart failure.

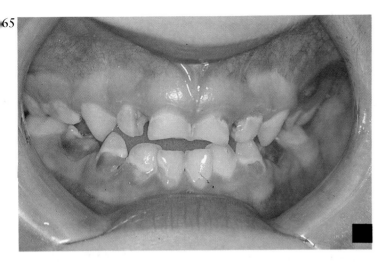

65 In any patient with infective endocarditis, careful examination of the teeth should be made since infection such as caries may be important.

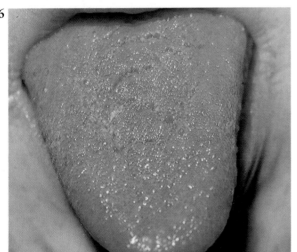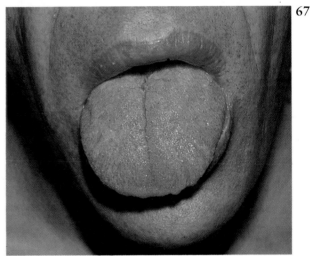

66 & 67 Macroglossia may be seen in Down's syndrome (**66**), amyloidosis and acromegaly (**67**). Down's syndrome is characteristically associated with atrioventricular septal defects and amyloidosis is an important cause of restrictive heart disease.

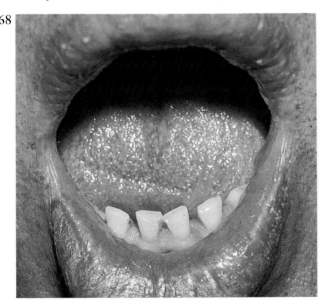

68 Overgrowth of the mandible leads to separation of the teeth in patients with acromegaly. Acromegaly is associated with diabetes and hypertension; rarely it may be associated with heart-muscle disease.

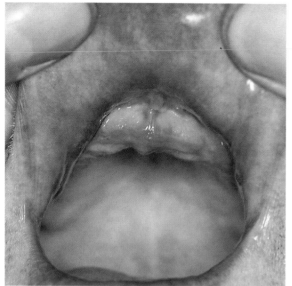

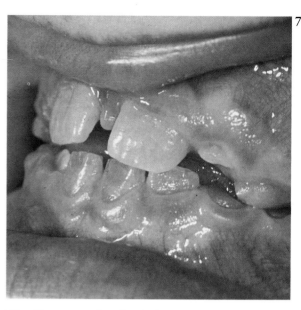

69 Evidence of Addison's disease should be sought in those with hypotension. In such patients, pigmentation on the buccal mucosa may be seen.

70 Dentogenesis imperfecta is the dental manifestation of osteogenesis imperfecta and is associated with aortic root disease. There is gross erosion of the deciduous dentition and discolouring of the permanent dentition.

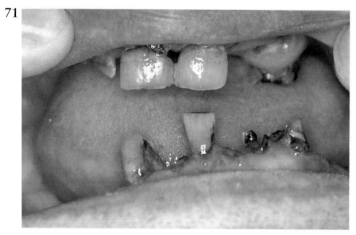

71 Scurvy may lead to high output cardiac failure and typically causes swollen, inflamed spongy gums with tooth loss.

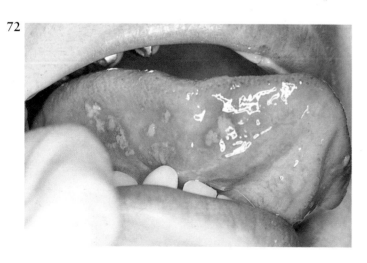

72 Mouth ulcers are a non-specific manifestation of virus infections which in this case was associated with a viral myocarditis.

THE HANDS

73–76 Clubbing may occur in acyanotic conditions such as infective endocarditis (**73**) but is more frequently associated with cyanotic congenital heart disease. Various degrees of clubbing may be seen in cyanotic individuals ranging from mild (**74**) to severe (**75, 76**). Severe clubbing has a drumstick type appearance.

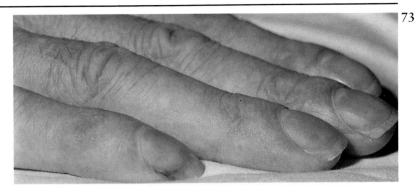

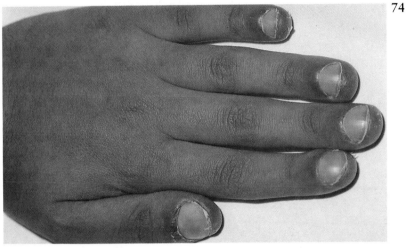

77-81 The physical stigmata of infective endocarditis include splinter haemorrhages which may be multiple (**77**) or single and large (**78**), Osler's nodes which may be single (**79**) or multiple (**80**). Rarely, non-specific dusky discoloration of fingers may be evident (**81**).

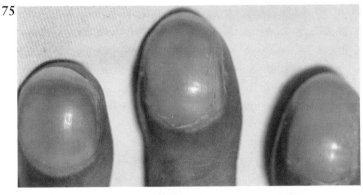

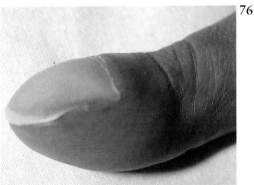

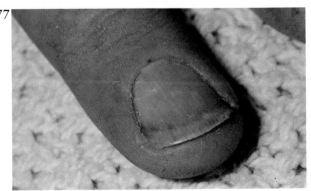

79

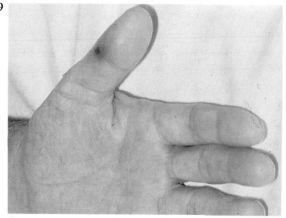

80

81

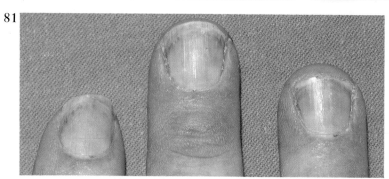

82

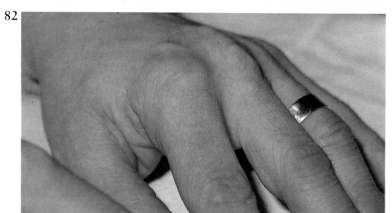

82 Tendon xanthomas may involve the hand in hyperlipidaemia.

83

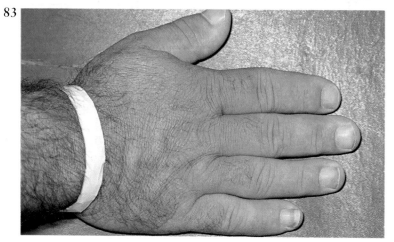

83 Broadening of the digits and the palm of the hand is a classical feature of acromegaly.

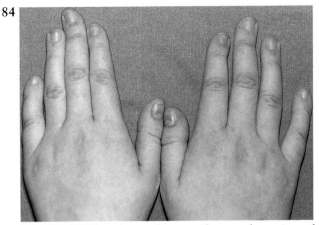

84 In Williams' syndrome (hypercalcaemia of infancy), classically there is a short little finger. Hypercalcaemia is associated with a supravalvular aortic stenosis.

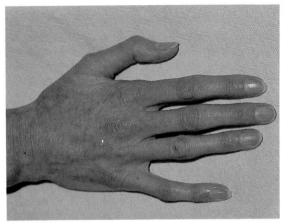

85 Arachnodactyly is a classical feature of Marfan's syndrome.

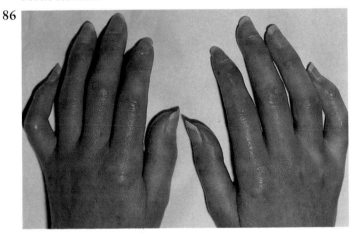

86 The immunologically mediated connective tissue diseases such as scleroderma and systemic sclerosis may be associated with coronary small vessel disease and pericardial disease. In this example, the hands of a patient with scleroderma are seen. Notice that they are swollen with tapering of the digits and infarcts around the nail bed.

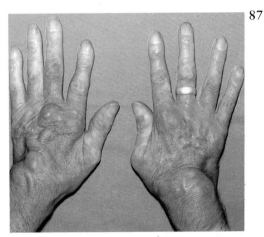

87 Rheumatoid arthritis, which is associated with pericardial disease, causes subluxation of the joints and ulnar drift.

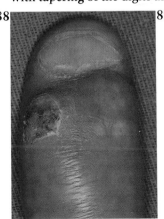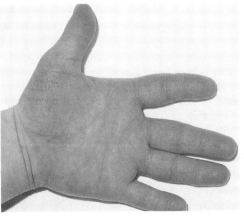

88 Hyperuricaemia is a weak risk factor for coronary disease and tophi may be seen involving the digits.

89 The hand in Down's syndrome shows short stubby fingers and a single transverse crease. Down's syndrome is often associated with serious congenital heart disease such as pulmonary stenosis, Fallot's tetralogy and atrioventricular septal defect.

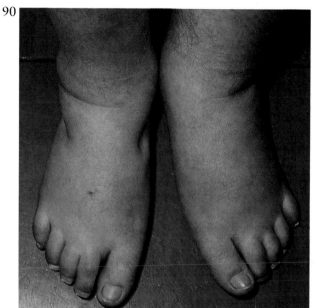

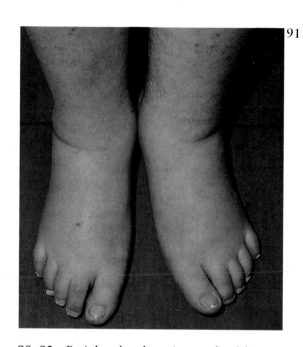

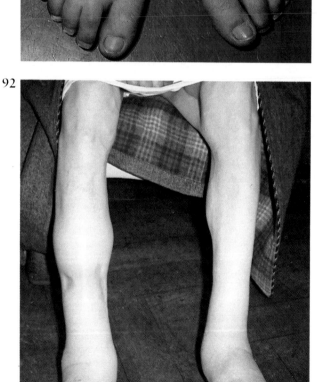

90–92 Peripheral oedema is a cardinal feature of right heart failure and although it may occur in other conditions, heart failure must always be excluded. Typical oedema (**90**) will pit on pressure (**91**) and the presence of oedema may hide the gross loss of muscle bulk due to cardiac cachexia (**92**).

93 Myxoedema may be associated with heart disease, particularly pericardial effusions and sinus bradycardia. The swelling in the legs must be differentiated from heart failure.

94 Whilst clubbing is most typically present in the hands, it may also occur in the feet in patients with cyanotic congenital heart disease.

95 In Eisenmenger patent ductus arteriosus, although clubbing of the feet may be present the hands are relatively spared.

96–98 In patients with infective endocarditis it is as important to examine the feet as the hands for the presence of typical pathognomonic features such as splinter haemorrhages. A large splinter haemorrhage is present in the great toe (**96**) which then grows out over the next six to eight weeks (**97**). Dermal infarcts may occur from septic emboli (**98**).

93
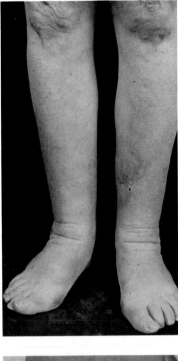

94
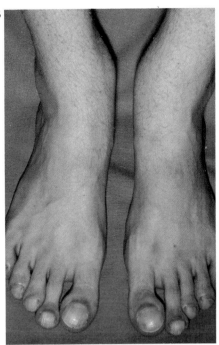

95
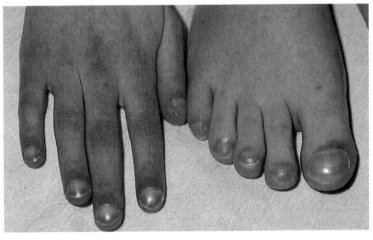

96
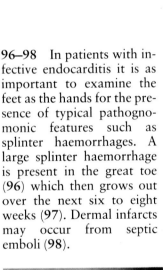

97
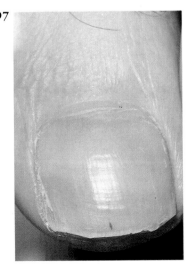

98
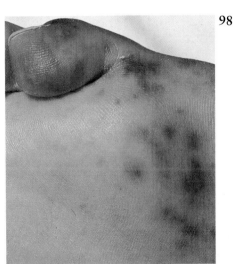

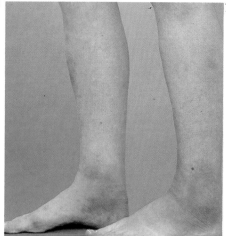

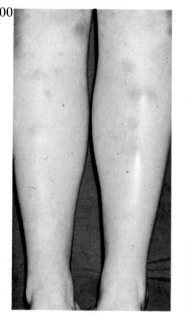

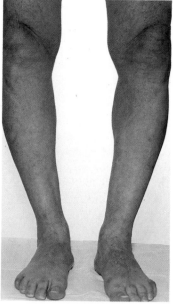

99 Rheumatic fever causing an acute arthropathy is rare in the western hemisphere but is common in developing countries.

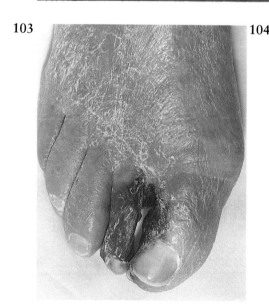

100 A rare cause of cardiomyopathy or complete heart block is cardiac sarcoid. There may be no cutaneous features or it may be manifested as erythema nodosum in which there are raised discrete round patches on the anterior shin.

101 Paget's disease is a very rare cause of high output cardiac failure. In this case there is bowing of the tibia.

102 Friedreich's ataxia shown here as pes cavus may cause specific heart-muscle diseases. Patients may die of either a dilated or hypertrophic cardiomyopathy.

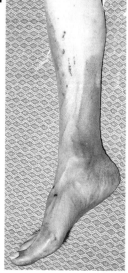

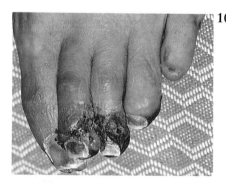

103–105 Arterial diseases of the leg may be embolic usually from either a cardiac source (**103**) or atherosclerotic disease of the major arterial vessels (**104**). Small vessel disease (e.g. systemic lupus erythematosus) may lead to digital gangrene (**105**).

106 & 107 Deep vein thrombosis causing a warm, swollen, painful leg is important in any patient with cardiac disease, but particularly following acute myocardial infarction. Deep vein thrombosis may lead to an acute pulmonary embolism or the insidious development of pulmonary hypertension. Venography (**107**) will demonstrate the presence of venous thrombosis.

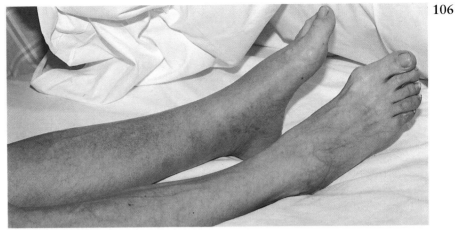

106

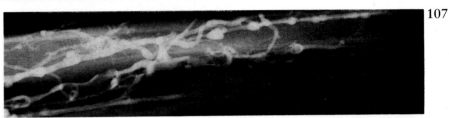

107

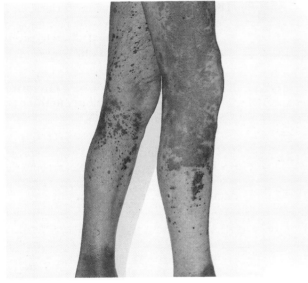

08

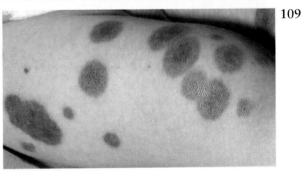

109

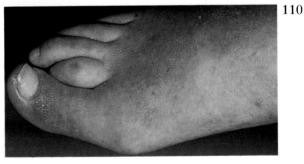

110

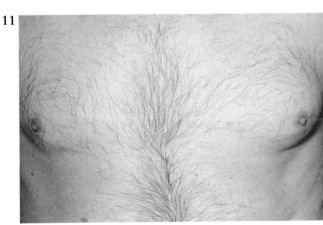

11

108–111 Drug reactions are important, particularly in patients with infective endocarditis on very large doses of antibiotics, and may be manifested as Henoch–Schölein purpura (**108**), erythema multiforme (**109**) and other forms of vasculitis. Treatment with thiazide diuretics may cause acute gout (**110**), and treatment with spironolactone may cause gynaecomastia (**111**).

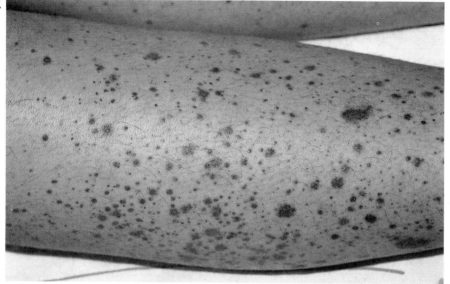

112 Polyarteritis nodosa may present with myocardial infarction and is typically associated with widespread systemic involvement causing a vasculitic skin rash often seen on the legs; there is, however, usually involvement of other organs such as the kidney.

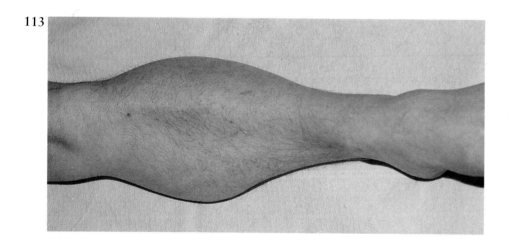

113 Muscular dystrophies are commonly associated with heart-muscle diseases. There may be muscle wasting or as in this case of late onset Duchenne's dystrophy (Becker's disease), there is marked calf hypertrophy.

THE RETINA

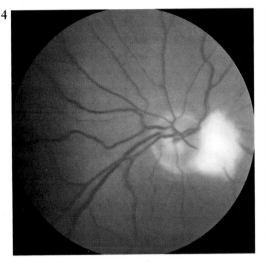

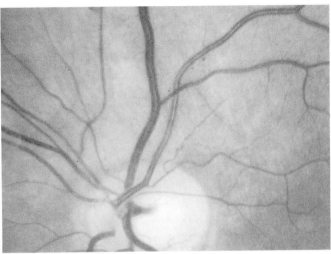

114 Normal optic fundus. There are medullated fibres seen in this normal fundus.

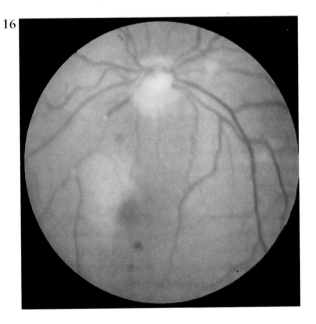

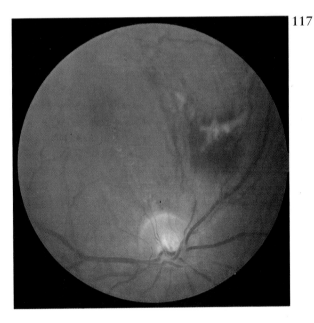

115–117 The hypertensive changes in the retina include silver wiring of the arteries (**115**), arteriovenous nipping and haemorrhages and exudates; these may be localised (**116**) or there may be extensive areas of flame shaped haemorrhages (**117**).

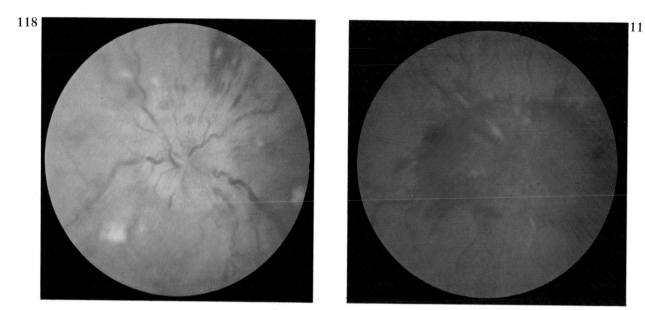

118 & 119 The most severe form of hypertensive retinopathy is papilloedema; the optic fundus is raised and oedematous (**118**) and usually there are extensive areas of haemorrhages and exudates (**119**). Other causes of papilloedema in patients with heart disease include hypercapnoea in cor pulmonale and Eisenmenger's syndrome.

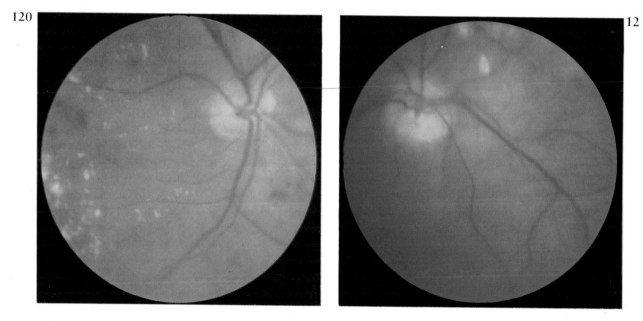

120–122 Diabetic retinopathy is very strongly associated with the presence of heart disease. The typical features of diabetic retinopathy include cotton wool spots and microaneurysms in background retinopathy (**120**). The later development of new vessels occurs (**121**) and in the most severe forms, there are extensive areas of new vessel formation with large areas of haemorrhages (**122**); this patient has undergone photocoagulation.

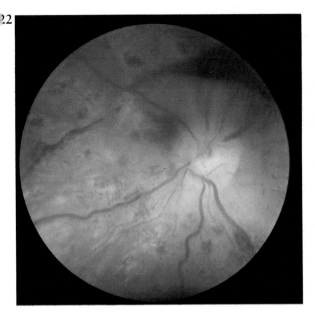

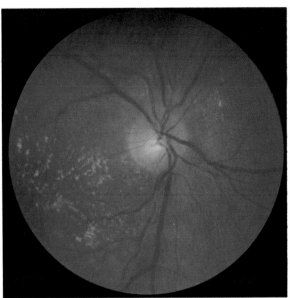

123 In hyperlipidaemic patients, the retinal fundus may show cholesterol deposits. These appear as white dots on the left hand side of the image.

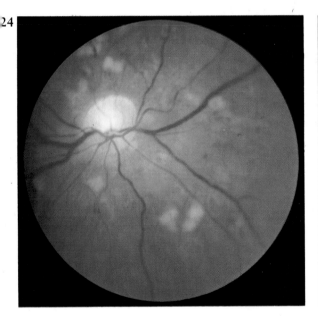

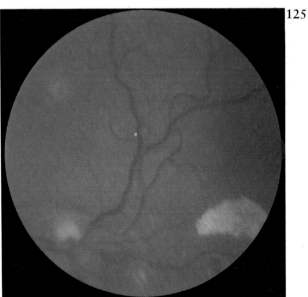

124 In scleroderma there may be widespread soft exudates seen in the retina.

125 Very rarely angina may be due to hyperviscosity and the cause of this should be sought. This retinal photograph is from a patient with multiple myeloma who presented with angina. There are areas of retinal infarction due to poor perfusion.

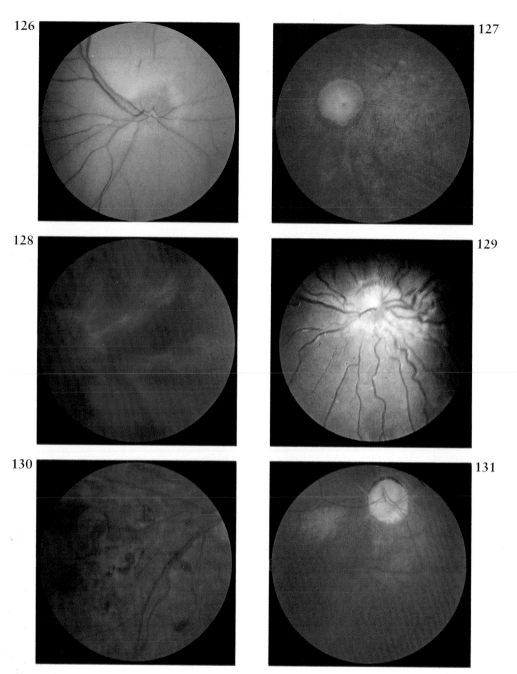

126–128 Emboli to the retina may occur from the heart or great vessels. In central retinal artery occlusion the retinal arterioles are attenuated with a pale and oedematous retina (**126**) and in the late phase there will be loss of vasculature (**127**). Retinal artery occlusion must be distinguished from retinal vein occlusion (**128**) in which there are multiple haemorrhages with swelling of the optic disc; retinal vein occlusion may occur in diabetic patients, but is rarely seen in patients with heart disease.

129 Coarctation of the aorta will lead to tortuosity of the vessels in the upper part of the body and this may be visible in the retina.

130 Choroid retinitis may appear in patients with viral illnesses particularly due to the cytomegalovirus and toxoplasmosis infections; this may be associated on rare occasions with a viral myocarditis. The features of choroid retinitis include abnormalities of pigmentation.

131 Retinitis pigmentosa may be seen in Refsum's syndrome in which cardiac sudden death is a common occurrence.

2. CLINICAL EXAMINATION OF THE CARDIOVASCULAR SYSTEM

Clinical examination of the cardiovascular system is historically divided into examination of the arterial pulse, the jugular venous pulse, the cardiac impulse and finally auscultation. Auscultation of the heart should include study of the first and second heart sounds followed by any additional sounds and finally the presence of systolic, diastolic or continuous murmurs.

THE ARTERIAL PULSE

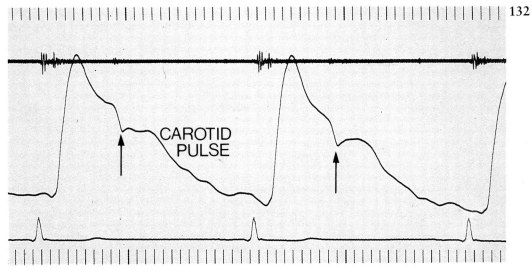

132 The normal arterial pulse has a rapid upstroke to a peak followed by a dicrotic notch (arrow) representing aortic valve closure.

133

134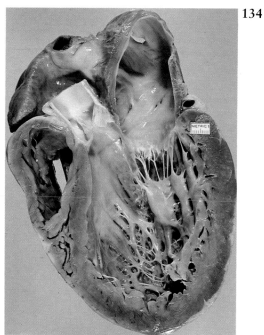

135

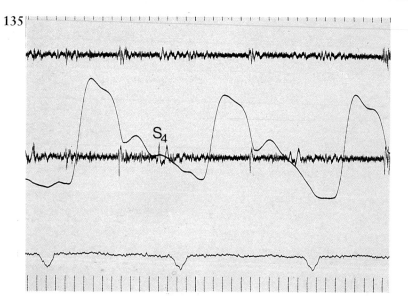

S_4

133–136 The pulse in the failing left ventricle is of small volume and at the end stage may show pulsus alternans. Dilated cardiomyopathy is an important cause of heart failure causing a dilated left ventricle (**133, 134**). Typically the pulse in this condition is of small volume and ill sustained (**135**). When the patients develop left ventricular failure, evidence of pulsus alternans (alternating small [1] and large [2] beats) may be present which is best elicited by sphygmomanometry (**136**); in this particular example the underlying cause of heart failure was aortic valve disease.

136

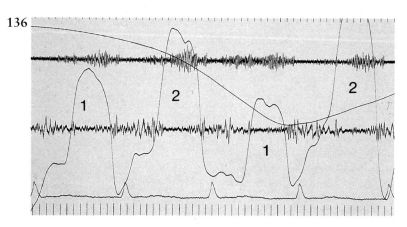

1 2 2

1

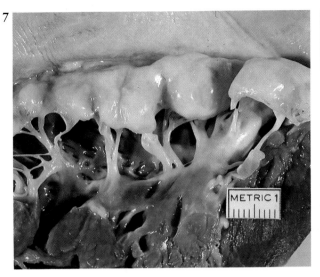

137–140 The pulse in significant mitral regurgitation is characteristically brisk and ill sustained. An important cause of mitral regurgitation is the floppy regurgitant mitral valve (**137**, **138**). There is increased surface area of the valve leaflets producing a scalloped appearance with focal fibrous thickening of the leaflets and ruptured chordae tendineae. A floppy, non-regurgitant mitral valve is shown viewed from the left atrium (**138**) where there is only slightly increased leaflet surface area with some focal thickening of the leaflets. The pulse in sinus rhythm (**139**) and atrial fibrillation (**140**) is ill sustained with a rapid upstroke. The phonocardiograms show a systolic murmur and a third heart sound.

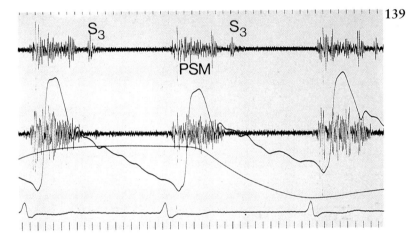

139

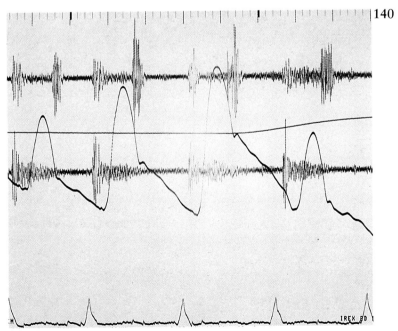

140

141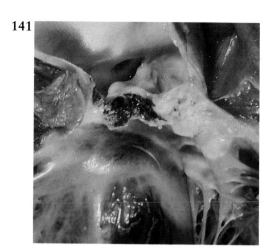

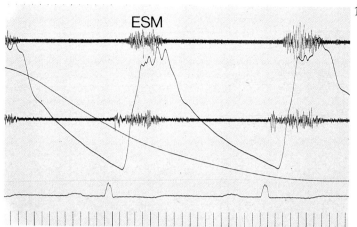

ESM

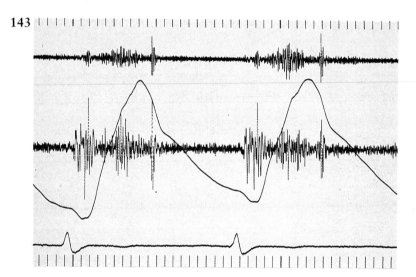

143

141–144 Aortic stenosis is characteristically associated with a slow rising pulse. A deformed and calcified valve leading to severe aortic stenosis is shown in **141**. In mild cases the pulse may be normal, but as aortic stenosis increases (**142**) there is a slight reduction in the upstroke of the pulse which becomes much more marked as the stenosis becomes more severe (**143**). The thrill over the carotids, particularly in adolescents, causes a coarse flutter (arrows) of the carotid trace (**144**).

144

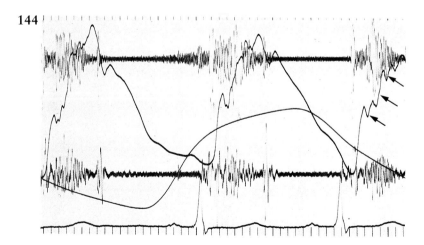

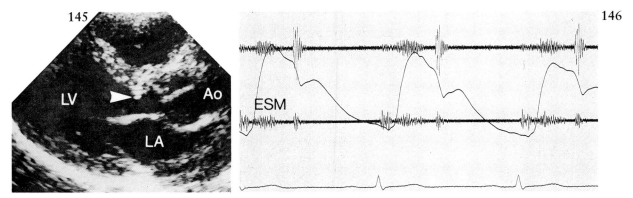

145 & 146 Subaortic stenosis is often associated with a normal pulse. It is most easily demonstrated on echocardiography as a discrete subaortic membrane (arrow, 145); the pulse is not slow rising and there is an ejection systolic murmur (146).

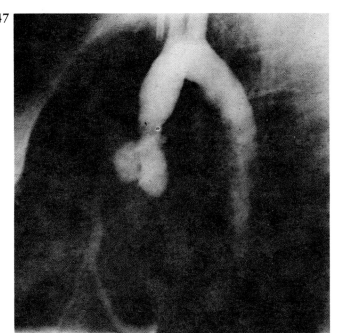

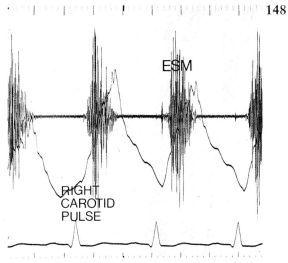

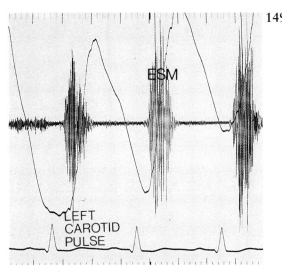

147–149 Supravalvular aortic stenosis is characteristically associated with inequality of the carotid pulses. Supravalvular aortic stenosis may be demonstrated on angiography as a waist above the aortic valve (147). The two carotids have been recorded separately; the right (148) has a slow rise with coarse fluttering representing a thrill and the left (149) is much less obviously slow rising.

150

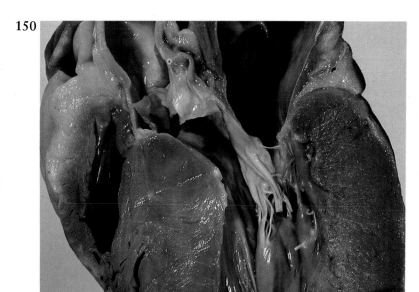

METRIC 1

150–152 Hypertrophic cardio-myopathy causes a jerky pulse which should be distinguished from the slow rising pulse of aortic stenosis. **150** shows a long axis section in hypertrophic cardiomyo-pathy in which both septum and left ventricular free wall are markedly hypertrophied and the outflow tract is narrow. An area of white, thickened endocardium overlies the bulging septum due to contact of the anterior leaflet of the mitral valve (contact lesion). The pulse in sinus rhythm is rapidly rising with a mid-systolic collapse (arrow, **151**). Post extrasystolic potentiation of the pulse is a characteristic feature. In atrial fibrillation following a long R-R interval there is more pronounced mid-systolic collapse (arrow) and a louder systolic murmur (**152**).

151

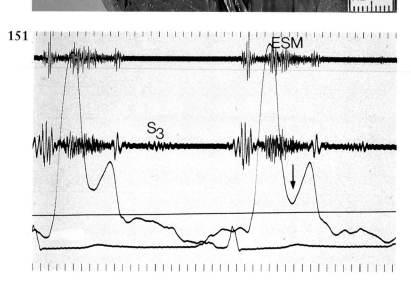

ESM

S_3

152

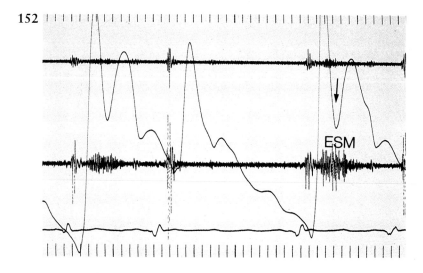

ESM

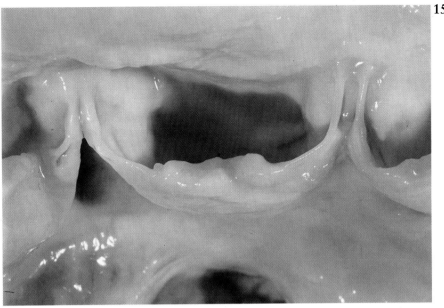

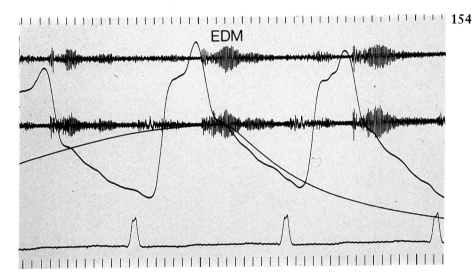

153 & 154 In aortic regurgitation the pulse is collapsing. In this example of aortic regurgitation due to ankylosing spondylitis, the valve cusps are shortened and thickened (**153**). The pulse (**154**) is of large volume and collapsing (waterhammer pulse, Corrigan sign).

155

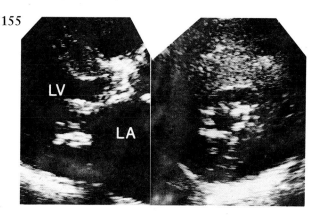

155 & 156 Mixed aortic stenosis and regurgitation is common in rheumatic heart disease which can be demonstrated on echocardiography (**155**) showing thickening of the aortic and mitral valves with left ventricular hypertrophy. The pulse will provide a guide to the dominant lesion and in this case is slow rising, but of large volume suggesting both severe aortic stenosis and regurgitation (**156**).

156

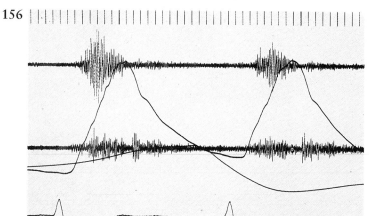

15

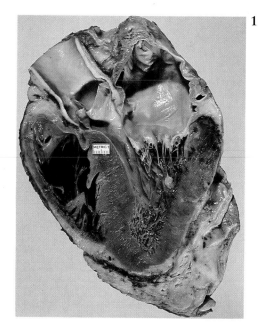

158

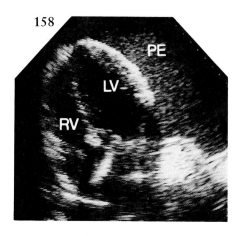

15

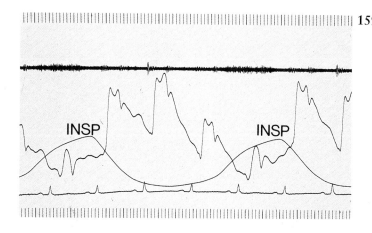

157–159 Pericardial disease may cause pulsus paradoxus. **157** shows a long axis section through the heart in acute myelomonocytic leukaemia with a thickened, white pericardium. Thickening of the pericardium or pericardial effusion can be demonstrated using cross sectional echocardiography (**158**); this case shows a clotted post-operative pericardial effusion. Pulsus paradoxus (**159**) is not paradoxical but is an increase in the normal physiological response to respiration. There is a marked fall in the pulse volume and duration during inspiration.

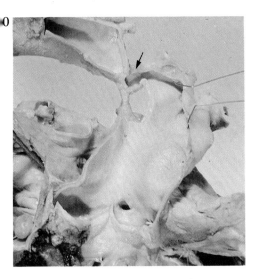

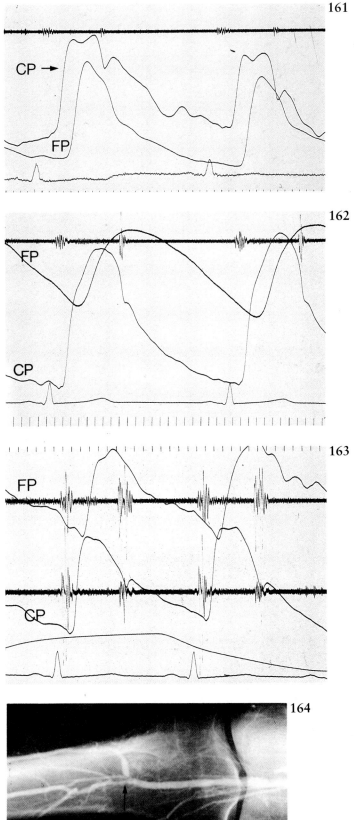

160–163 Coarctation of the aorta produces a reduction in the volume and delay of the femoral pulses. Coarctation of the aorta (arrow) is usually post-ductal (**160**) causing normal pulses in the arms and the neck but diminished femoral pulses. Normally (**161**) there is little delay between the carotid and femoral pulses, but this becomes marked in patients with coarctation of the aorta (**162**) in which the pulse is not only delayed, but is also very prolonged. Following correction of the coarctation the pulses return to normal (**163**).

164 Absence of pulses will occur in patients with peripheral vascular disease. The site of block or narrowing (arrow) may be demonstrated on angiography.

THE JUGULAR VENOUS PULSE

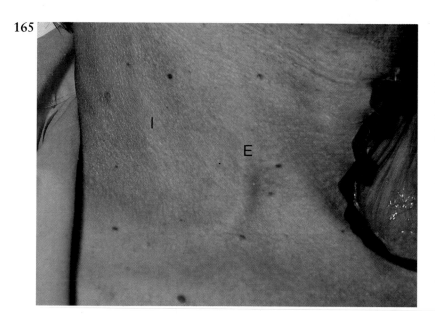

165 Examination of the venous pressure must differentiate the internal (I) from the external (E) jugular vein. For accurate measurement of the height of the venous pressure, and recording of the wave form, the internal jugular vein should be examined.

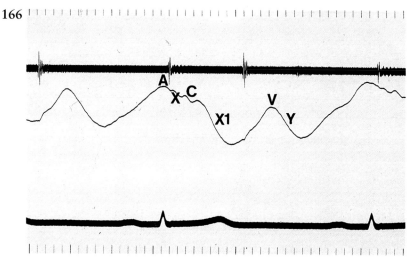

166 In a normal subject, the jugular venous pulse is only evident with the patient lying flat. On clinical examination it is only possible to visualise the 'A' and 'V' waves together with the 'X' and 'Y' descent. Using a surface transducer, the 'C' wave can also be seen which divides the 'X' descent into the 'X' and 'X1' descent.

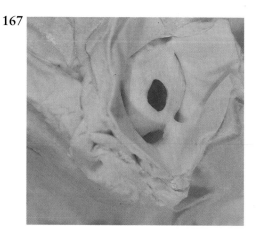

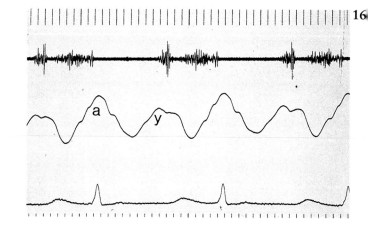

167-172 The 'a' wave of the jugular venous pressure will be accentuated in those conditions that cause an increased right ventricular filling pressure; this is most commonly due to right ventricular hypertrophy from conditions such as pulmonary valve stenosis or pulmonary hypertension. A stenosed pulmonary valve viewed from above is shown in **167**. In mild pulmonary stenosis the 'a' wave is accentuated (**168**) but barely exceeds the 'v' wave; in contrast, in severe pulmonary stenosis, the 'a' wave is dominant (**169**), and following an atrial extrasystole (arrow) with a short P-R interval the 'a' wave becomes even more prominent (**170**). Right ventricular hypertrophy due to pulmonary hypertension cannot be distinguished from pulmonary stenosis on examination of the jugular venous pulse alone; this patient with an Eisenmenger atrioventricular septal defect also shows a prominent 'a' wave (**171**). Compression of the right ventricle by lesions involving the left ventricle, particularly hypertrophic cardiomyopathy, will similarly cause accentuation of the 'a' wave of the jugular venous pressure (Bernheim effect) (**172**).

169

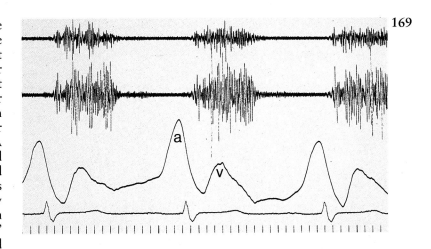

170

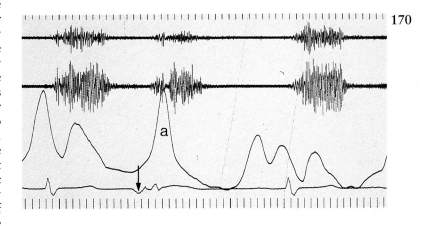

171

172

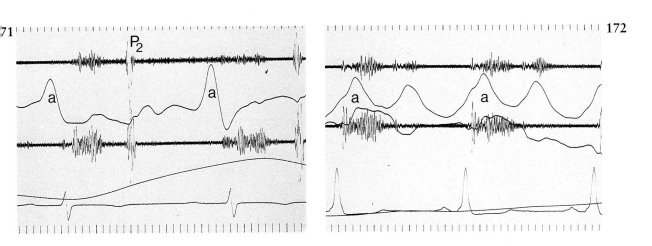

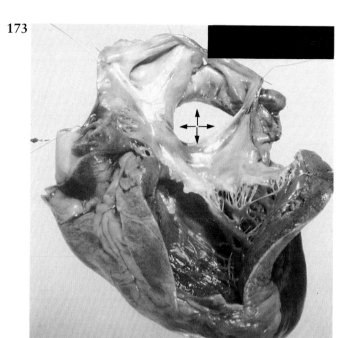

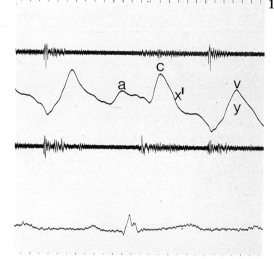

175

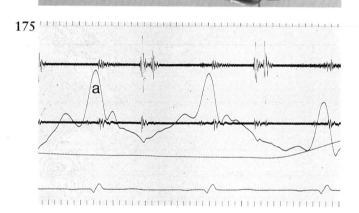

173–175 Defects of the atrial septum may result in an increase in right atrial pressure with balanced pressures between the left and right atrium. A secundum atrial septal defect (arrowed) viewed from the left side is shown in **173**. The venous pressure in secundum atrial septal defect will show normal 'a' and 'v' waves, but a deep x descent (**174**); with the development of pulmonary hypertension, the 'a' wave will become prominent (**175**).

176 & 177 Characteristic abnormalities of the venous pressure in tricuspid stenosis may include a dominant 'a' wave if the patient is still in sinus rhythm, but typically there is a reduced y descent. A cross sectional echocardiogram in rheumatic mitral and tricuspid valve disease (arrow) is shown in **176**; the jugular venous pressure shows that in atrial fibrillation the 'a' wave is absent and there is a reduced y descent (**177**).

176

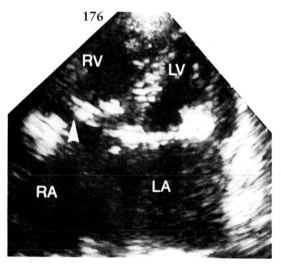

17

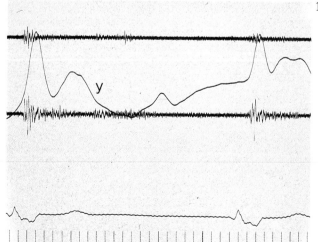

178–181 In tricuspid regurgitation, the venous pressure is dominated by the presence of a systolic wave. **178** shows a dilated tricuspid ring in pulmonary hypertension secondary to left heart disease; this resulted in severe tricuspid regurgitation. In sinus rhythm, there is a marked systolic wave (SW), but the 'a' wave is accentuated (**179**); in atrial fibrillation the 'a' wave will be absent and a single systolic wave is all that is seen (**180**). The x descent is slow (**181**).

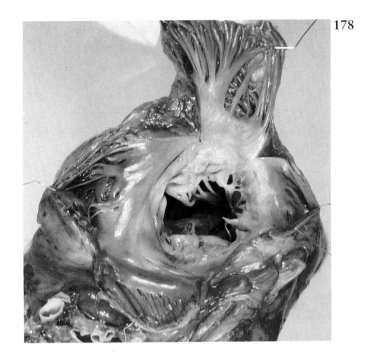

178

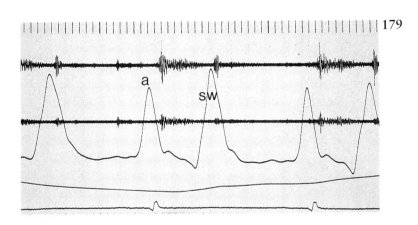

179

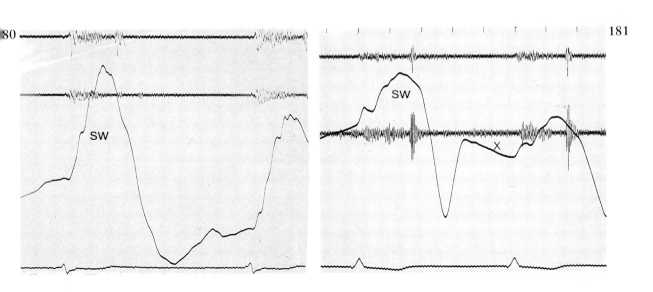

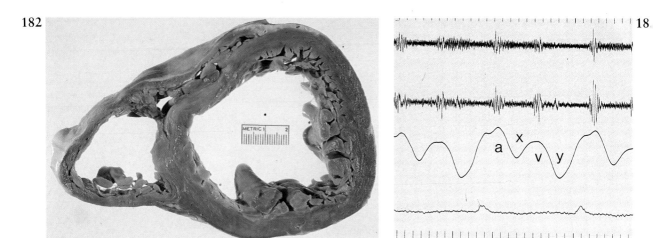

182 & 183   Dilatation of both ventricles may occur in dilated cardiomyopathy (**182**) and this will cause an increased right ventricular filling pressure resulting in a dominant 'a' wave and a poor x descent (**183**).

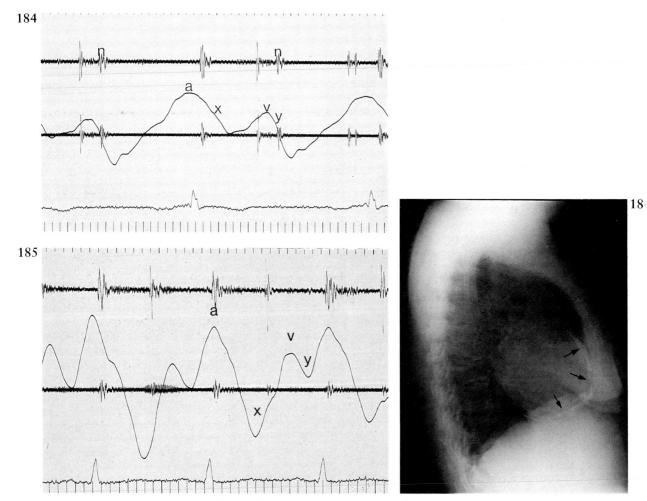

184–186   Constrictive pericarditis will restrict right ventricular filling causing a rapid y descent in the venous pulse which is coincidental with the pericardial knock (n) (**184**); this has to be differentiated from cardiac tamponade in which a rapid x descent is dominant (**185**). Constrictive pericarditis is often associated with pericardial calcification (arrows), which can be seen on the chest x-ray (**186**), and thickening of the pericardium may be seen on cross sectional echocardiography. The physical signs may be mixed in the effusive–constrictive form of pericardial disese.

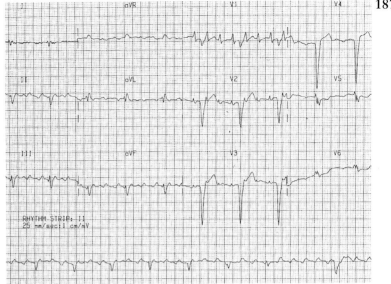

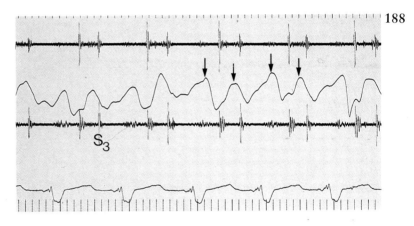

187 & 188 In atrial flutter (**187**) the venous pressure is dominated by the presence of flutter waves (arrows, **188**). In this patient the atrial flutter precipitated the development of heart failure and consequently a third heart sound is seen on the phonocardiogram.

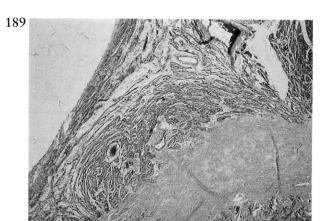
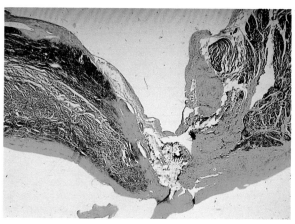

191

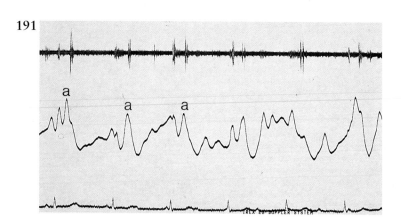

189–191 Atrial contraction against a closed tricuspid valve will result in cannon waves. Complete heart block is often idiopathic when the normal atrioventricular node (**189**) undergoes vacuolisation with destruction of the nodal tissue (**190**). The jugular venous pressure will show cannon 'a' waves when atrial contraction occurs against a closed tricuspid valve (**191**).

192

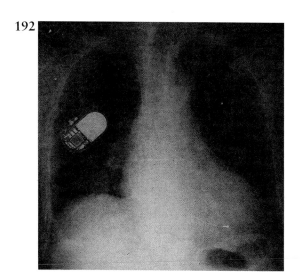
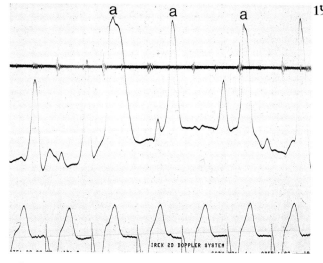

192 & 193 Following insertion of a cardiac pacemaker (**192**) the presence of cannon 'a' waves will still persist in ventricular inhibited pacing systems (**193**).

THE CARDIAC IMPULSE

194 The normal cardiac impulse is felt in the left fourth or fifth intercostal space in the mid-clavicular line. It consists of an A wave which is not felt in normal subjects, an upstroke to the E point which is felt, followed by systolic retraction to the O point; the rapid filling phase to an F point is again not felt.

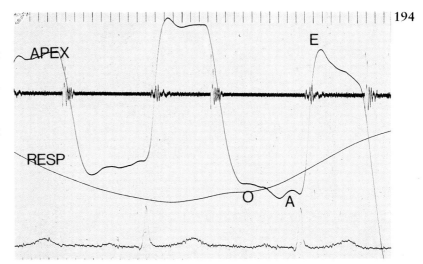

195–198 In concentric left ventricular hypertrophy, the cardiac impulse is displaced outward and has a thrusting character causing a sustained apex cardiogram. A specimen with severe left ventricular hypertrophy due to calcific aortic stenosis is shown in **195**. Where the left ventricular hypertrophy is mild, the apex will not be sustained (**196**). This can be compared with severe left ventricular hypertrophy where the left ventricular apex is very obviously sustained (arrow, **197**). This is an important clinical point that can be used to differentiate mild from severe aortic stenosis. When left ventricular hypertrophy is very severe, there will be a prominent 'a' wave which will be palpable (**198**).

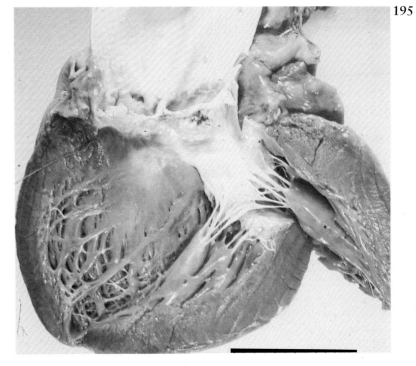

196

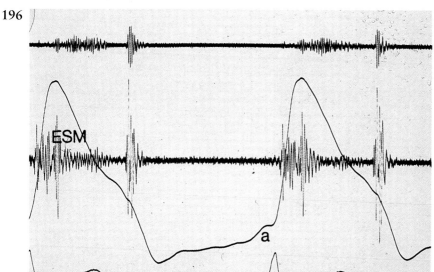

ESM

a

197

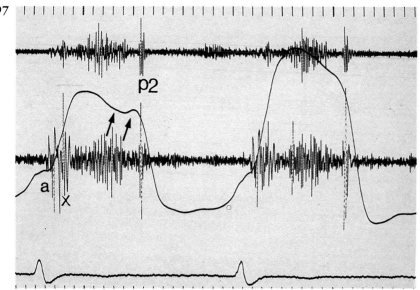

p2

a
x

198

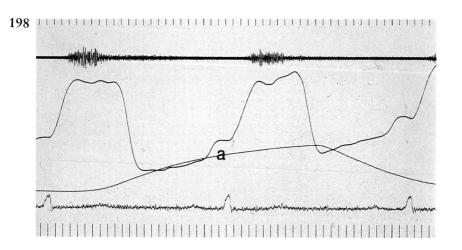

a

195–198 In concentric left ventricular hypertrophy, the cardiac impulse is displaced outward and has a thrusting character causing a sustained apex cardiogram. A specimen with severe left ventricular hypertrophy due to calcific aortic stenosis is shown in **195**. Where the left ventricular hypertrophy is mild, the apex will not be sustained (**196**). This can be compared with severe left ventricular hypertrophy where the left ventricular apex is very obviously sustained (arrow, **197**). This is an important clinical point that can be used to differentiate mild from severe aortic stenosis. When left ventricular hypertrophy is very severe, there will be a prominent 'a' wave which will be palpable (**198**).

199–201 In left ventricular dilatation the apex is not only displaced outwards and downwards, but in contrast to left ventricular hypertrophy is heaving in character. A transverse section of the ventricles in left ventricular cavity dilatation is shown in **199**. Where left ventricular dilatation is mild to moderate the apical impulse may not be displaced, but typically will be hyperdynamic. In severe aortic regurgitation causing more marked left ventricular dilatation a sustained apical impulse will be felt which is also hyperdynamic (**200**). In severe chronic mitral regurgitation a prominent 'a' wave will also be palpable in the presence of a sustained hyperdynamic cardiac impulse (**201**).

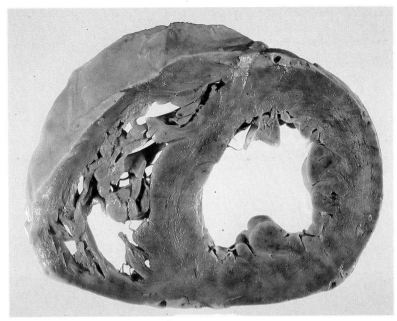

199

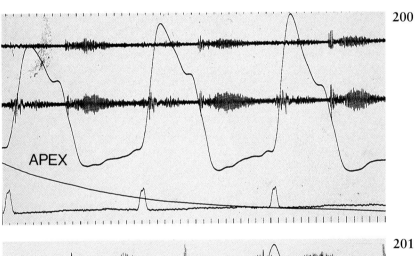

APEX

200

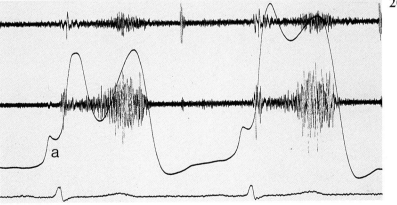

a

201

202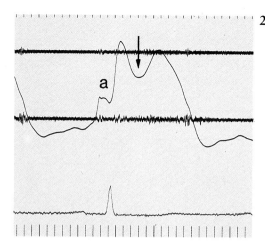

202 & 203 Characteristically hypertrophic cardiomyopathy is associated with a palpable 'a' wave and a mid-systolic dip in the apical impulse. A long axis echo view of the heart in hypertrophic cardiomyopathy is shown in **202**. There is gross left ventricular hypertrophy, more marked in the septum than in the free wall. The apical impulse has a very prominent 'a' wave and there is a mid-systolic collapse (arrow) in the sustained left ventricular impulse (**203**).

204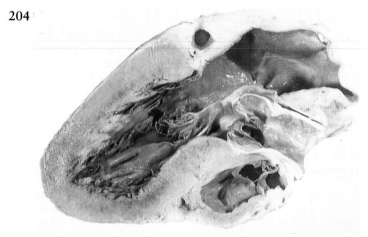

205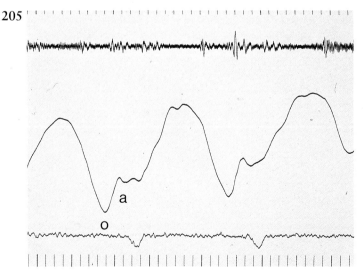

204 & 205 The characteristic feature of restrictive cardiomyopathy is the dip and plateau of the left ventricular filling pressure which can be demonstrated on the apex cardiogram A long axis echo cut section of the heart in amyloidosis is shown in **204**. The heart is enlarged and the myocardium has a rubbery consistency. Apex cardiogram shows a prominent 'a' wave which occurs on a plateau after the o point (**205**).

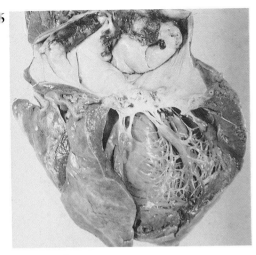

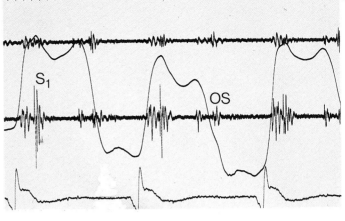

207

206 & 207 In the examination of the cardiac impulse in mitral stenosis it is important to feel for a tapping impulse indicating a loud first heart sound and also to look for the presence of right ventricular hypertrophy representing pulmonary hypertension. Rheumatic mitral stenosis with a mural left atrial clot is shown in **206**. The apical impulse in pure mitral stenosis will not be displaced but will be tapping in quality which can be timed with a loud first heart sound (**207**).

208–211 Evidence of left ventricular damage in patients following acute myocardial infarction may be obtained by examining the cardiac impulse. The left ventricular cavity following an extensive transmural antero-apical myocardial infarction is shown in **208**. The entire anterior wall in thinned and the overlying endocardium is densely thickened and white. The apex cardiogram following a large anterior infarct will show a prominent 'a' wave (**209**). A left ventricular aneurysm may be inferred from the presence of a very tall 'a' wave representing 50% of the overall apical displacement together with late systolic motion; the dyskinetic segment may be felt in the anterior chest (**210**). Following the development of widespread damage, left ventricular cavity dilatation will occur with outward and downward displacement of the apex and cannot be distinguished from other causes of left ventricular dilatation (**211**); in this example there is a palpable third heart sound.

208

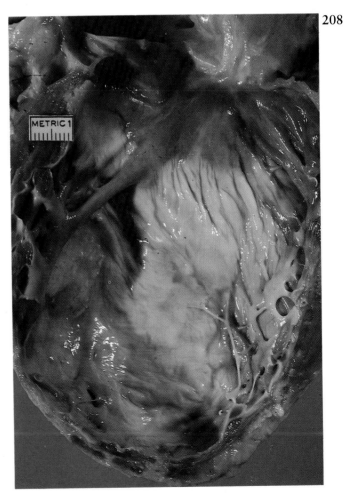

209

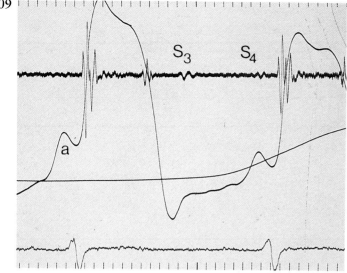

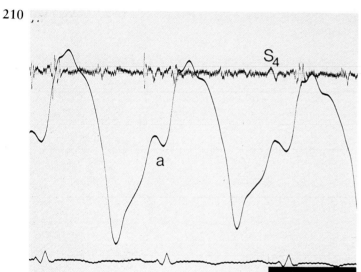

210

208–211 Evidence of left ventricular damage in patients following acute myocardial infarction may be obtained by examining the cardiac impulse. The left ventricular cavity following an extensive transmural antero-apical myocardial infarction is shown in **208**. The entire anterior wall in thinned and the overlying endocardium is densely thickened and white. The apex cardiogram following a large anterior infarct will show a prominent 'a' wave (**209**). A left ventricular aneurysm may be inferred from the presence of a very tall 'a' wave representing 50% of the overall apical displacement together with late systolic motion; the dyskinetic segment may be felt in the anterior chest (**210**). Following the development of widespread damage, left ventricular cavity dilatation will occur with outward and downward displacement of the apex and cannot be distinguished from other causes of left ventricular dilatation (**211**); in this example there is a palpable third heart sound.

211

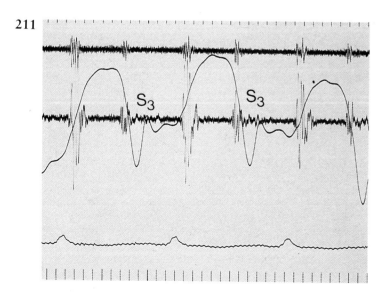

212–216 Normally the right ventricular impulse is not felt but in the presence of right ventricular hypertrophy, a right ventricular heave along the left sternal border will be evident. An example of right ventricular hypertrophy is shown in **212**. In mild right ventricular hypertrophy, the systolic impulse is accentuated, but the 'a' wave is inconspicuous (arrow, **213**). With more severe right ventricular hypertrophy the 'a' wave becomes prominent and the impulse is sustained (arrows, **214**). Normally the right ventricular impulse precedes the left ventricular apical impulse; however, when there is interventricular communication as in a ventricular septal defect, the two will occur in synchrony (**215**). When tricuspid regurgitation occurs the impulse becomes large in volume (**216**).

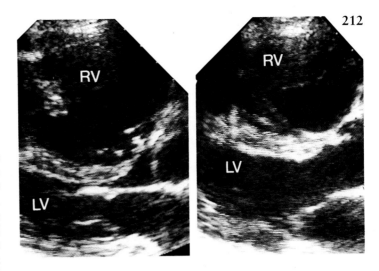

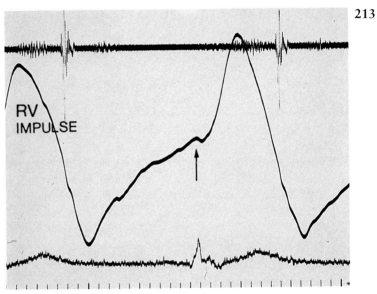

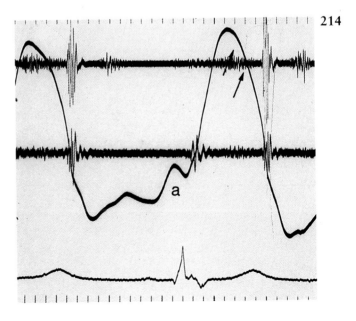

215

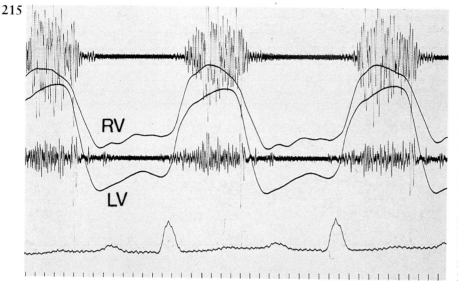

RV

LV

216

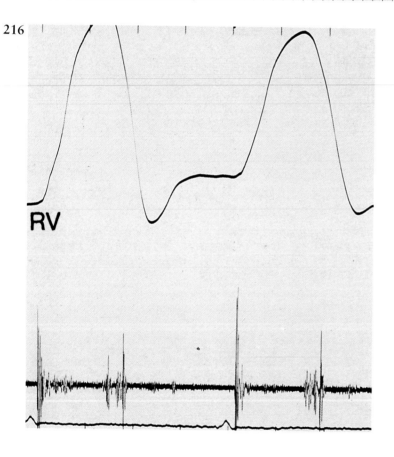

RV

212–216 Normally the right ventricular impulse is not felt but in the presence of right ventricular hypertrophy, a right ventricular heave along the left sternal border will be evident. An example of right ventricular hypertrophy is shown in **212**. In mild right ventricular hypertrophy, the systolic impulse is accentuated, but the 'a' wave is inconspicuous (arrow, **213**). With more severe right ventricular hypertrophy the 'a' wave becomes prominent and the impulse is sustained (arrows, **214**). Normally the right ventricular impulse precedes the left ventricular apical impulse; however, when there is interventricular communication as in a ventricular septal defect, the two will occur in synchrony (**215**). When tricuspid regurgitation occurs the impulse becomes large in volume (**216**).

HEART SOUNDS

217–222 There is a wide variation in the normal heart sounds. The third and fourth heart sounds may be physiological in the younger patient. The first heart sound has two components—mitral closure followed by tricuspid closure (**217**). The second heart sound is made up by the aortic and pulmonary components (**218**). On expiration aortic and pulmonary closure are narrowly split, but on inspiration the pulmonary component is delayed. In young patients it is common to hear a physiological third heart sound which disappears in early adult life (**219**). A characteristic feature of the physiological third heart sound is that its intensity varies with respiration (**220**). In athletes, physiological third and fourth heart sounds may be present in older subjects (**221,222**).

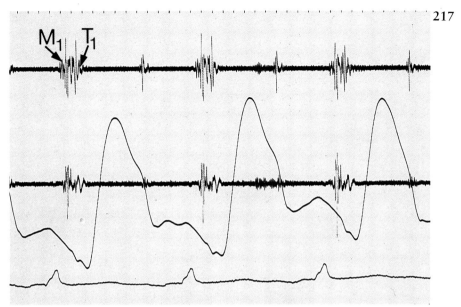

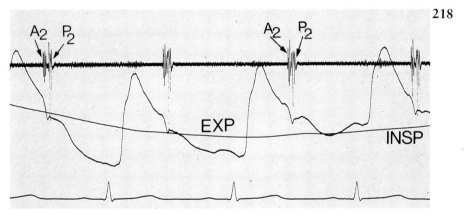

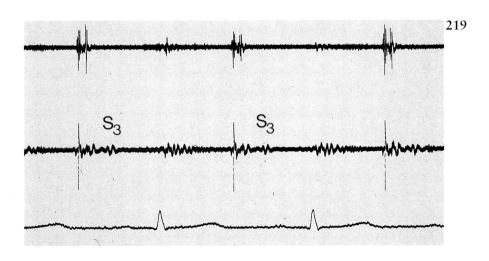

220

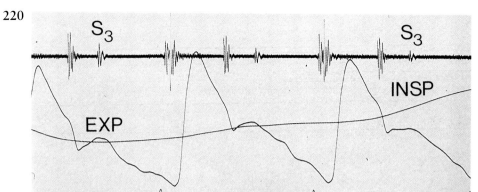

S_3　S_3　INSP　EXP

221

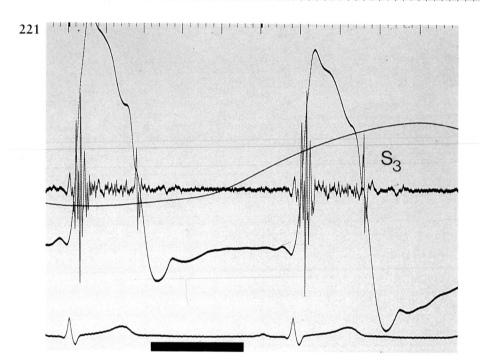

S_3

222

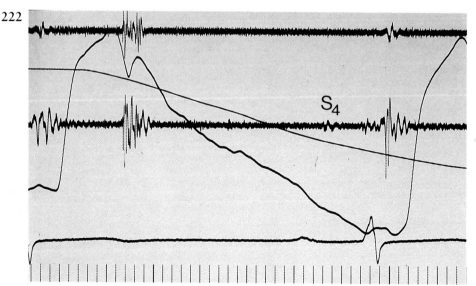

S_4

217–222 There is a wide variation in the normal heart sounds. The third and fourth heart sounds may be physiological in the younger patient. The first heart sound has two components—mitral closure followed by tricuspid closure (**217**). The second heart sound is made up by the aortic and pulmonary components (**218**). On expiration aortic and pulmonary closure are narrowly split, but on inspiration the pulmonary component is delayed. In young patients it is common to hear a physiological third heart sound which disappears in early adult life (**219**). A characteristic feature of the physiological third heart sound is that its intensity varies with inspiration (**220**). In athletes, physiological third and fourth heart sounds may be present in older subjects (**221,222**).

223–225 A loud first heart sound may be heard in patients with a short P-R interval because the mitral valve is closing at a higher left atrial pressure (e.g. in patients with pre-excitation syndrome). **223** shows a penetrating atrioventricular bundle in the Wolff–Parkinson–White syndrome which causes a short P-R interval, a delta wave and a dominant R wave in V1 in Wolff–Parkinson–White syndrome type A (**224**). The effect of this short P-R interval is an accentuated first heart sound (S1) (**225**).

223

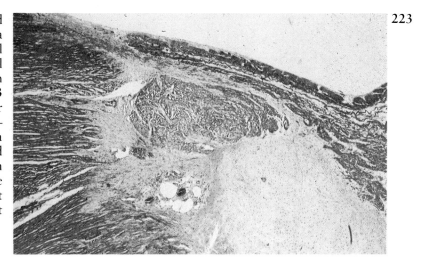

224

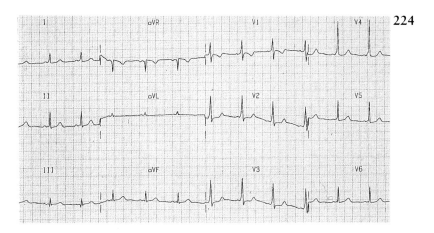

225

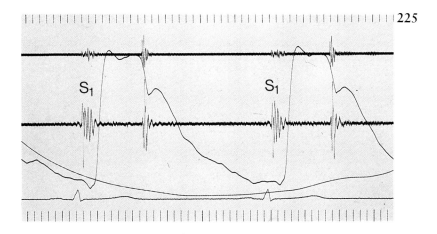

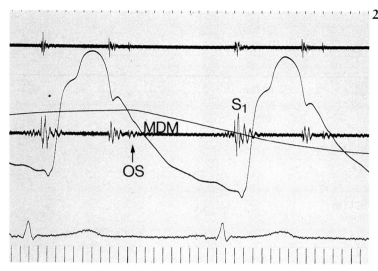

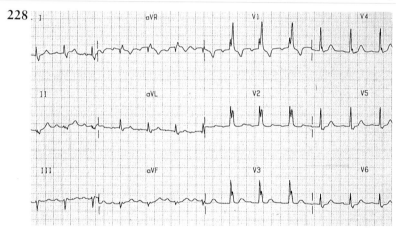

226 & 227 The mechanism of the loud first heart sound in mitral stenosis is similar to that of the short P-R interval, that is a high left atrial pressure at the time of mitral closure. A stenosed rheumatic mitral valve (arrows) is shown in **226**. In mitral stenosis there is a loud first heart sound (**227**) and in addition there is evidence of an opening snap and mid-diastolic murmur.

228

228 & 229 In contrast, a soft first heart sound occurs when the P-R interval is prolonged (**228**). The importance of the P-R interval in determining the amplitude of the first heart sound is shown in **229**; on the left there is a long P-R interval with a soft first heart sound; on the right a paced beat which occurs shortly after atrial contraction ('a' wave in the upstroke of the apex cardiogram) will cause a loud first heart sound.

229

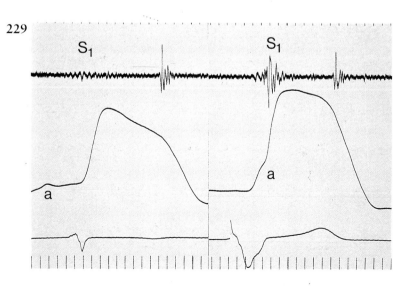

230–232 Causes of an increased left ventricular end-diastolic pressure (such as a dilated left ventricle and aortic stenosis) will result in a soft first heart sound. A long axis echo cut of dilated cardiomyopathy is shown in **230**. In this patient there was a quiet first heart sound (**231**) which was further diminished by the presence of left bundle branch block. Likewise in aortic stenosis, the high left ventricular end-diastolic pressure together with immediate partial closure movement of the mitral valve will also lead to a soft first heart sound (**232**).

230

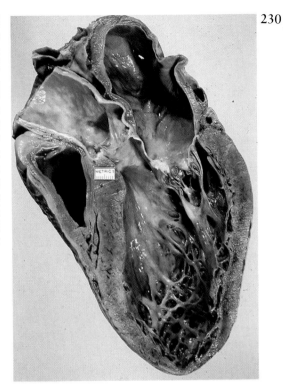

231

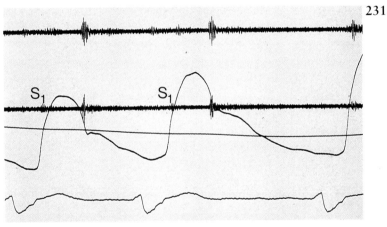

232

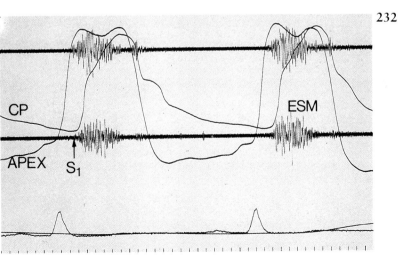

233

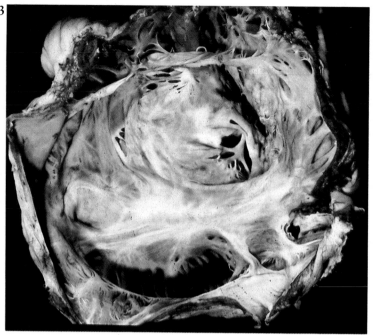

233–236 Splitting of the first heart sound is a characteristic feature of Ebstein's anomaly. **233** shows the deformed tricuspid valve with an atrialised right ventricle (AV) viewed from the right atrium. The cross sectional echocardiogram shows the atrialisation of the right ventricle and movement of the redundant and downwardly displaced tricuspid valve (arrows) in systole and diastole (**234,235**). Splitting of the first heart sound is clearly seen with delay of its tricuspid component (**236**). In addition, the characteristic added sounds are evident.

234

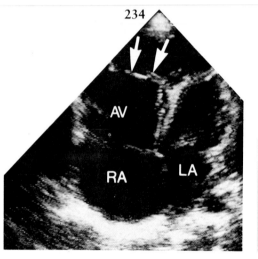

AV

RA   LA

235

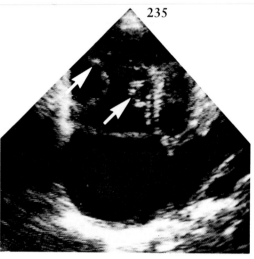

236

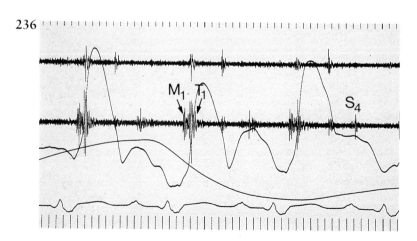

M_1 T_1 S_4

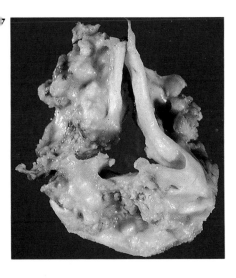

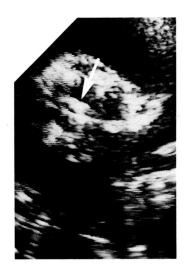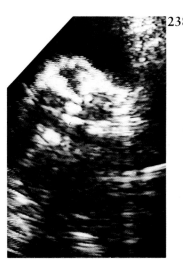

237–241 Delay and softening of the aortic component of the second heart sound characteristically occurs in moderate and severe aortic stenosis. A calcified degenerative three cuspid aortic valve is shown in **237**; this is clearly demonstrated using cross sectional echocardiography (**238**) which shows a thickened calcified immobile three cuspid valve (arrowed) (systole left, diastole right). Usually, in severe aortic stenosis, the aortic component of the second heart sound is delayed and often inaudible (**239**), though occasionally, even in severe aortic stenosis, a quiet delayed aortic component of the second heart sound may be heard (**240**). The timing of the second heart sound (arrow), even when inaudible can be demonstrated using M-mode echocardiography (**241**).

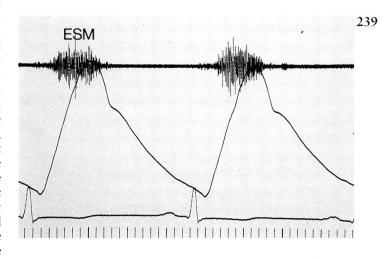

239

ESM

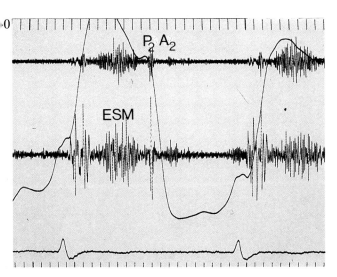

P_2 A_2

ESM

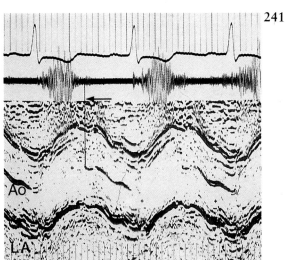

241

Ao

LA

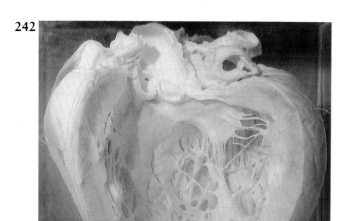

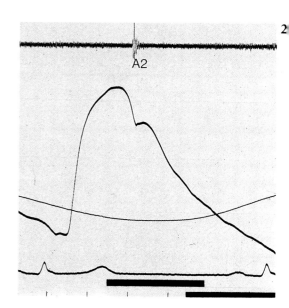

242 & 243 The commonest cause of a loud aortic component of the second heart sound is hypertension of at least moderate severity. **242** shows a dilated and hypertrophied left ventricle from malignant hypertension. The phonocardiogram demonstrates accentuation of the aortic component of the second heart sound (**243**).

244

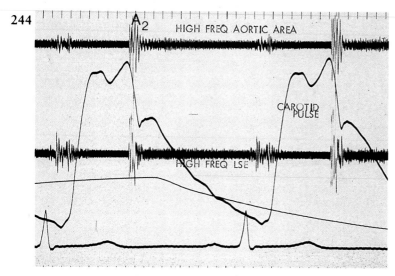

244 Occasionally patients with mitral valve prolapse also have aortic valve prolapse; this condition causes a loud aortic component of the second heart sound.

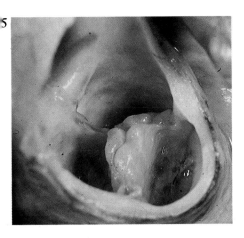

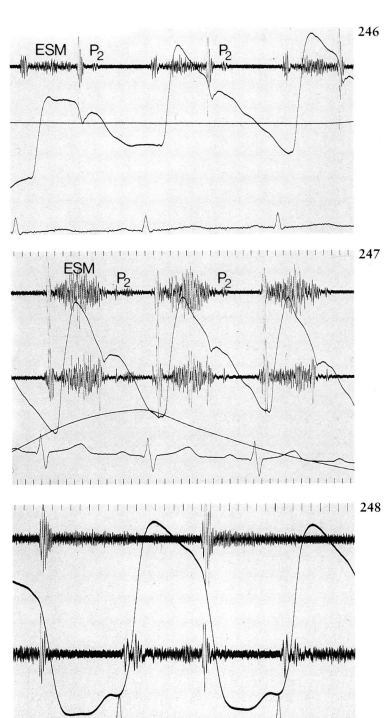

245–248 A soft and delayed pulmonary component of the second heart sound typically occurs in pulmonary stenosis. A stenosed pulmonary valve viewed from above is shown in **245**. In mild pulmonary stenosis the pulmonary component of the second heart sound is soft and delayed (**246**). With increasing severity, the murmur becomes louder and the pulmonary component of the second heart sound becomes further delayed, but still moves normally with respiration (**247**). In very severe pulmonary stenosis, or pulmonary atresia, the pulmonary component of the second heart sound is absent (**248**).

249

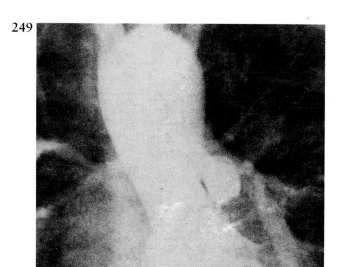

249 & 250 In Fallot's tetralogy the second heart sound is similar to that in pulmonary stenosis. A left ventricular angiogram (anteroposterior projection) is shown in **249**; there is a ventricular septal defect and severe pulmonary stenosis. The phonocardiogram shows a soft and delayed pulmonary component of the second heart sound (**250**).

250

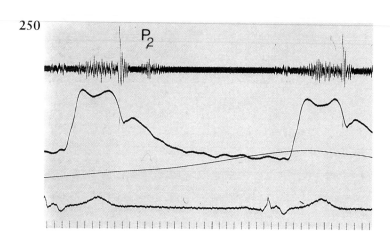

P₂

251

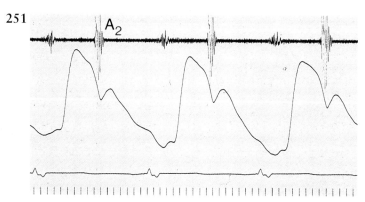

A₂

251 A single second heart sound may be due to an absent aortic component of the second heart sound as in severe aortic stenosis or an absent pulmonary component as in severe pulmonary stenosis. In more complex congenital conditions, the second heart sound may be single because of the relationship of the pulmonary valve to the chest wall so that pulmonary valve closure cannot be heard (e.g. transposition of the great arteries). The phonocardiogram in transposition of the great arteries will show a loud aortic component of the second heart sound since the aortic valve lies anteriorly, but the pulmonary component is not heard since it lies posteriorly thus leading to a single second heart sound.

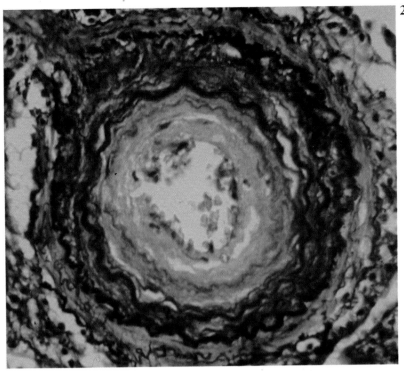

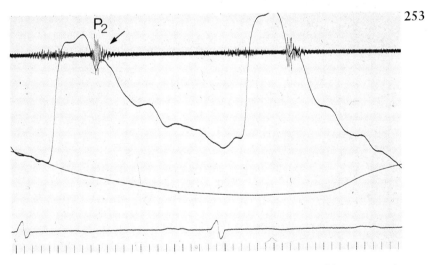

252 & 253 A loud pulmonary component of the second heart sound occurs in pulmonary hypertension. A histological section of the pulmonary artery in primary pulmonary hypertension is shown in **252**; there is splitting of the internal elastic lamina and fibrosis of the intima. In pulmonary hypertension of any cause the pulmonary component of the second heart sound is accentuated and often there is evidence of mild pulmonary regurgitation (early diastolic murmur arrow **253**).

254

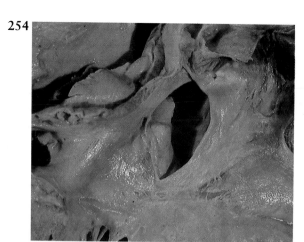

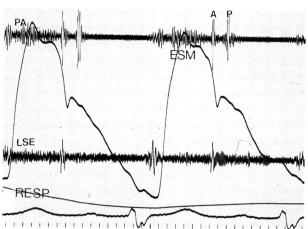

PA

A P

ESM

LSE

RESP

256

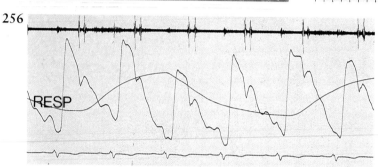

RESP

254–258 Fixed splitting of the second heart sound characteristically occurs in atrial septal defect. A secundum atrial septal defect viewed from the left side is shown in **254**; the second heart sound is widely split (**255**) and does not move with respiration (**256**). This must be differentiated from valvular pulmonary stenosis (**257**) and right bundle branch block (**258**) in which wide splitting of the second heart sound occurs but moves with respiration.

257

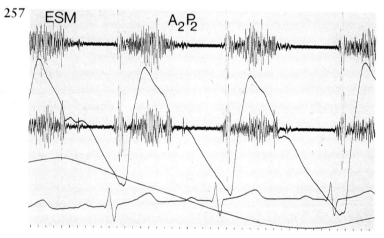

ESM $A_2 P_2$

258

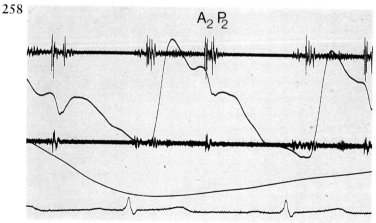

$A_2 P_2$

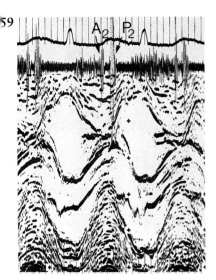

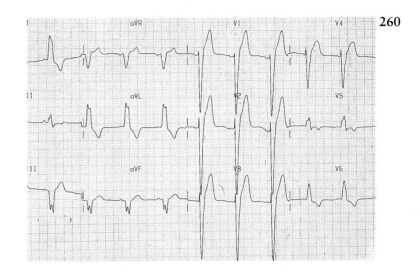

259 Wide splitting of the second heart sound may rarely occur because the aortic component is early rather than the pulmonary component being significantly delayed. When the duration of left ventricular ejection is shortened as in severe mitral regurgitation or ventricular septal defect, the aortic component of the second heart sound may occur early as in this example of severe mitral regurgitation.

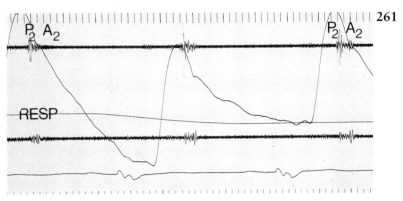

261

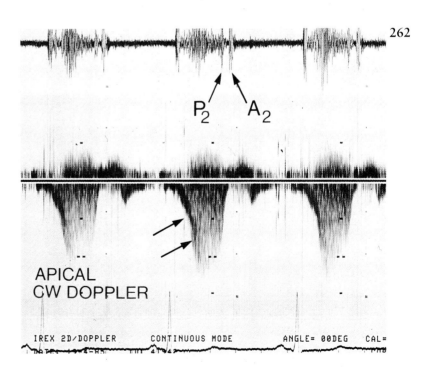

262

APICAL
CW DOPPLER

IREX 2D/DOPPLER   CONTINUOUS MODE   ANGLE= 00DEG   CAL=

260–262 Reversed splitting of the second heart sound must be differentiated from normal. In left bundle branch block (**260**) the aortic component of the second heart sound will be delayed so that in inspiration splitting will become reversed (**261**). In hypertrophic cardiomyopathy the left ventricular outflow tract obstruction results in prolongation of left ventricular ejection with reverse splitting. The aortic component of the second heart sound remains normal in intensity (**262**).

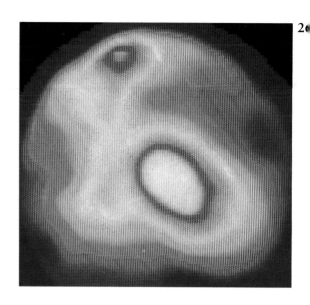

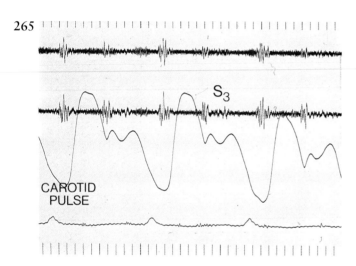

263–268 The third heart sound occurs at the time of rapid filling of the left ventricle and is a characteristic feature of heart failure. The fourth heart sound may also occur in patients with heart failure at the time of atrial systole; both third and fourth heart sounds occur when there is derangement of the diastolic properties of the left ventricle. A gated blood pool scan is shown (263 systole, 264 diastole) of a dilated poorly contracting left ventricle in heart failure. Auscultation at the apex reveals a third heart sound (265) and occasionally a fourth heart sound (266). The fourth heart sound can be timed with atrial systole on recordings of the venous pressure. When there is a tachycardia, summation of the third and fourth heart sounds (arrows) produces a typical gallop rhythm (267). Following an extrasystole, the third heart sound is diminished, but there is post extrasystolic potentiation of the fourth heart sound (268).

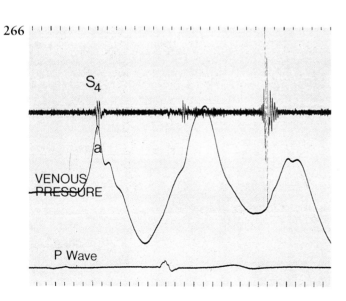

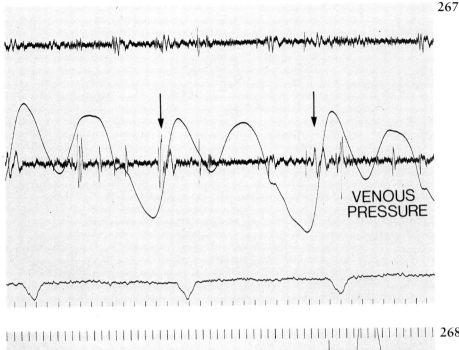

VENOUS
PRESSURE

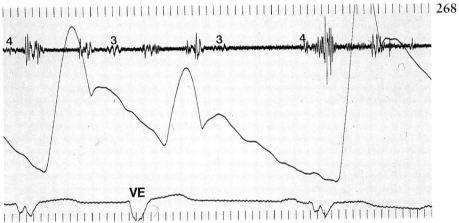

4   3   3   4

VE

269-272 Third and fourth heart sounds may occur in conditions other than heart failure. **269** shows an excised floppy redundant mitral valve with ruptured chordae causing severe mitral regurgitation. Both third (**270**) and fourth heart sounds (**271**) can be heard in non-rheumatic mitral regurgitation. In rheumatic mitral regurgitation, an opening snap (arrow) may still be present and precedes the third heart sound (**272**); note the F wave of the apex cardiogram is coincidental with the third heart sound.

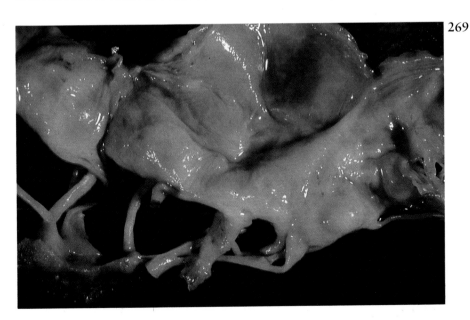

270

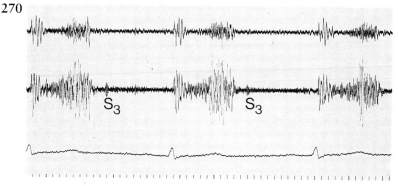

S_3 S_3

271

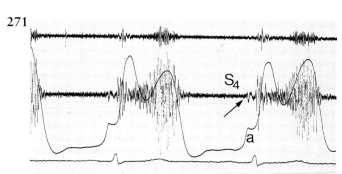

S_4

a

269-272 Third and fourth heart sounds may occur in conditions other than heart failure. **269** shows an excised floppy redundant mitral valve with ruptured chordae causing severe mitral regurgitation. Both third (**270**) and fourth heart sounds (**271**) can be heard in non-rheumatic mitral regurgitation. In rheumatic mitral regurgitation, an opening snap (arrow) may still be present and precedes the third heart sound (**272**); note the F wave of the apex cardiogram is coincidental with the third heart sound.

272

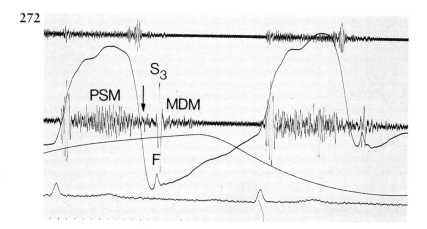

S_3

PSM   MDM

F

273

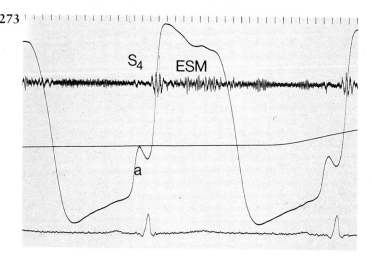

S_4 ESM

a

273 A fourth heart sound is a characteristic feature of hypertrophic cardiomyopathy.

274 & 275 Amyloid heart disease causes restriction of ventricular filling and is associated with the presence of a fourth heart sound. A long axis section of the heart in amyloidosis is shown in **274**. A fourth heart sound is heard on auscultation (**275**); rarely a third heart sound may also be heard.

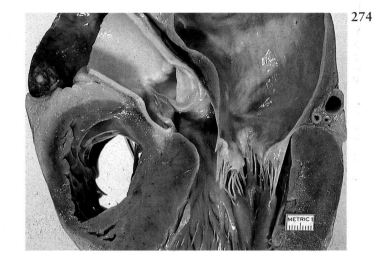

274

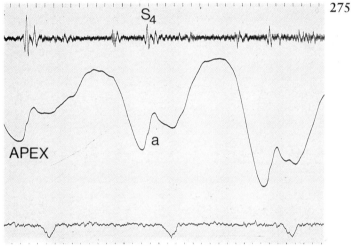

275

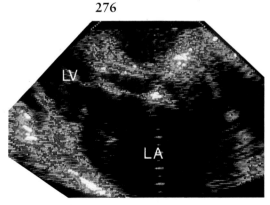

276

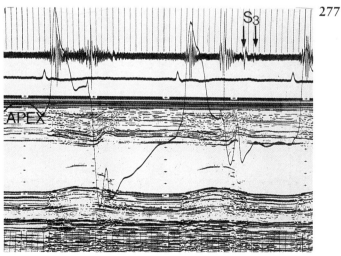

277

276 & 277 Restrictive cardiomyopathy is generally associated with impaired ventricular filling and characteristically a third heart sound occurs. A colour encoded cross sectional echocardiogram is shown (**276**) with gross enlargement of the left atrium and high intensity echoes in the left ventricular myocardium suggesting the presence of myocardial fibrosis. Simultaneous M-mode echocardiogram and phonocardiogram in the same patient (**277**) shows a poorly functioning hypertrophied left ventricle with right and left ventricular third heart sounds (arrowed).

81

278

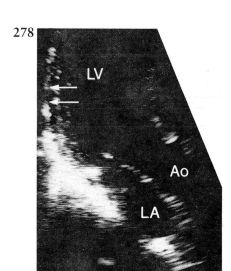

LV

Ao

LA

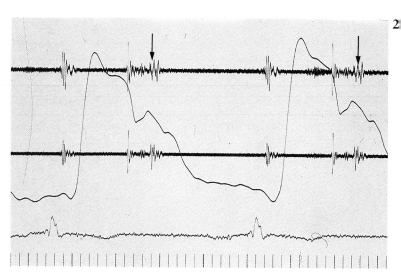

280

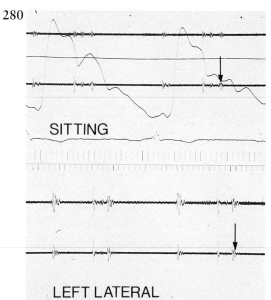

SITTING

LEFT LATERAL

278–280 Restrictive cardiomyopathy must be differentiated from constrictive pericarditis which produces a sound that is earlier in diastole than the third heart sound and is called a pericardial knock. **278** shows a thickened pericardium (arrows) demonstrated by cross sectional echocardiography. A pericardial knock (arrowed) can be seen (**279**) occurring about 40 milliseconds earlier than the third heart sound would be expected. A pericardial knock (arrowed) is usually only heard with the patient lying in the left lateral position and is often absent when the patient sits up (**280**).

281 & 282 Third and fourth heart sounds may also occur in patients following acute myocardial infarction who develop a left ventricular aneurysm. A gated blood pool image of a left ventricular aneurysm is shown in **281**. These are amplitude images and a large area of the apex is not contracting (in dark red on the image). Auscultation reveals both the third and fourth heart sounds (**282**).

281

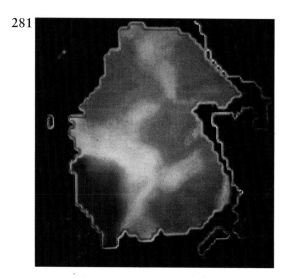

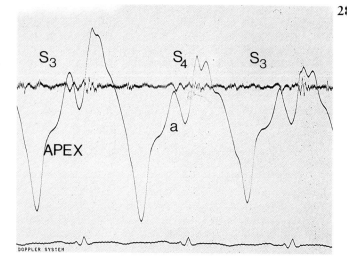

S_3

S_4

S_3

a

APEX

DOPPLER SYSTEM

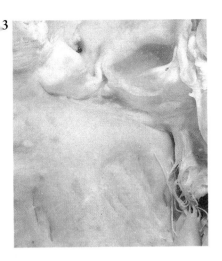

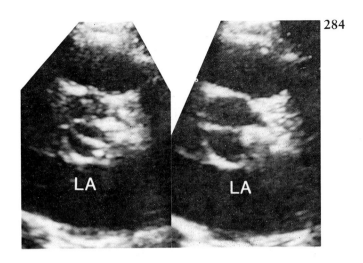

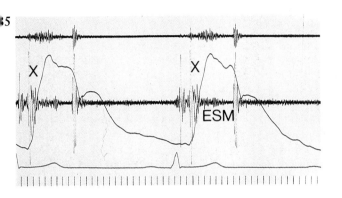

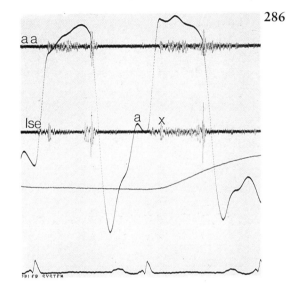

283–287 Systolic ejection clicks may arise early in systole from the aortic or pulmonary valves or occasionally the great arteries. A bicuspid non-stenotic aortic valve is shown in **283**. The presence of a bicuspid aortic valve is most easily demonstrated using cross sectional echocardiography (short axis parasternal view; systole right, diastole left, **284**). The presence of a systolic click (X) is unrelated to the severity of the obstruction and may be clearly evident even in the presence of only mild aortic stenosis (**285**) or even in the absence of any obstruction whatsoever (**286**). An ejection click from a bicuspid valve needs to be differentiated from the root click of a dilated aorta such as occurs in Fallot's tetralogy (**287**).

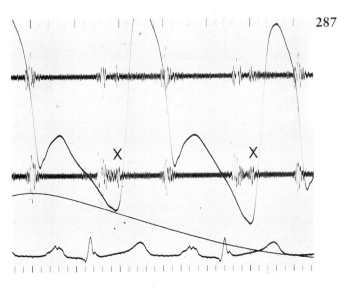

288

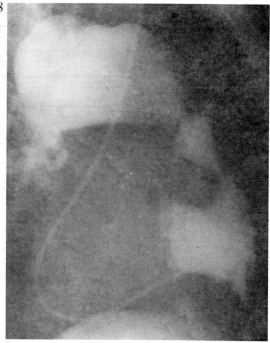

288–292 An ejection click in the pulmonary area is usually associated with valvular pulmonary stenosis but may arise from a deformed valve without significant obstruction. A right ventricular angiogram (**288**) (lateral projection) shows valvular pulmonary stenosis with post-stenotic dilatation. In mild pulmonary stenosis there is a soft ejection click (X) in the pulmonary area (**289**). A loud ejection click may still be present in severe pulmonary stenosis (**290**). This should be differentiated from an ejection click which occurs in the aortic root in patients with pulmonary atresia (**291**) and also differentiated from delayed tricuspid closure in right bundle branch block (**292**).

289

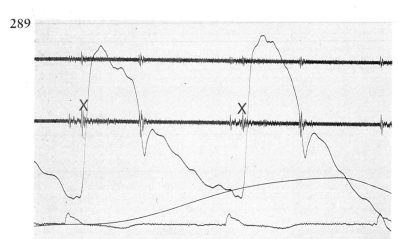

290

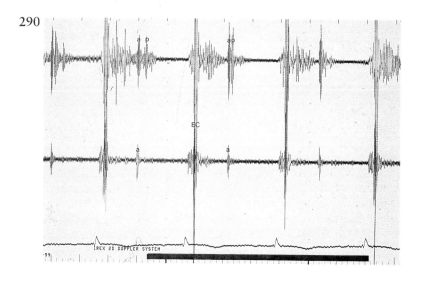

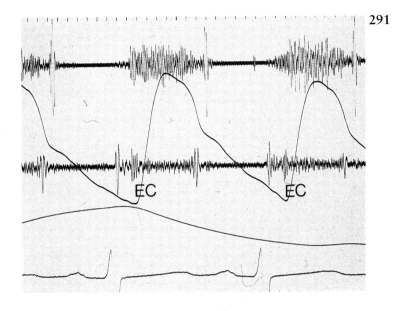

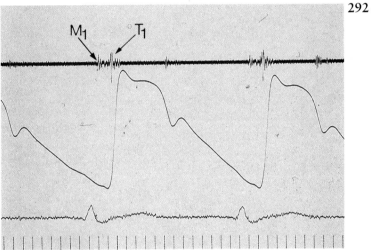

93

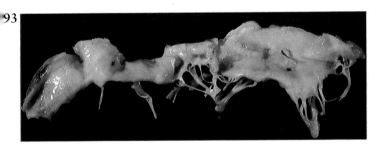

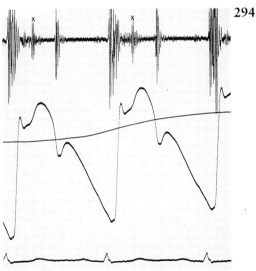

293 & 294 Late systolic clicks arise from the atrioventricular valve, the most frequent being the mitral valve. An excised floppy regurgitant mitral valve with rupture of the chordae tendineae is shown in **293**. The click (X) in mitral valve prolapse occurs in mid to late systole and may not be associated with a late systolic murmur (**294**). The clicks can occasionally be multiple.

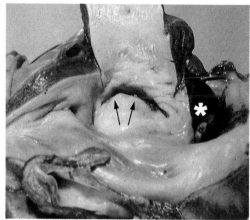
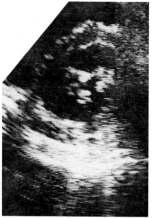
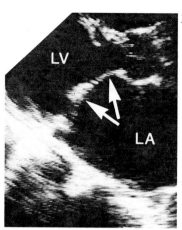

LV

LA

297

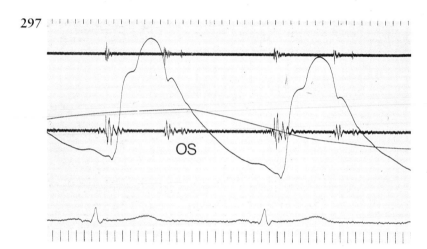

OS

298

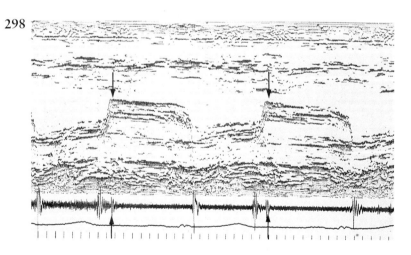

295–298 An opening snap occurs characteristically in rheumatic mitral valve disease. This is due to rapid 'checking' of the valve in diastole. A rheumatic stenosed mitral valve (arrowed) viewed from the left atrium is shown in **295**. There is also a clot (✱) in the left atrium. The domed and thickened valve (arrows) can be seen on cross sectional echocardiography (**296** right hand image) with reduction in mitral valve orifice (**296** left hand image). The opening snap occurs 70–120 milliseconds after aortic closure and its timing reflects the severity of stenosis; the earlier it occurs the more severe the stenosis (**297**). The opening snap (arrows) can be timed from the M-mode echocardiogram (**298**) and is coincidental with the rapid anterior motion of the anterior leaflet of the mitral valve (arrows).

299 & 300 In cardiac myxoma the presentation and physical signs may be similar to mitral stenosis. However, instead of an opening snap, there is a tumour 'plop' which must be differentiated from an opening snap. Left atrial myxoma is best demonstrated using cross sectional echocardiography which will show a large mass (✱) lying within the left atrium (**299**). The tumour plop (TP) occurs as the tumour moves from the left atrium into the left ventricle (**300**).

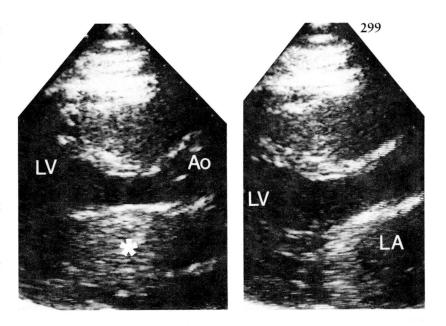

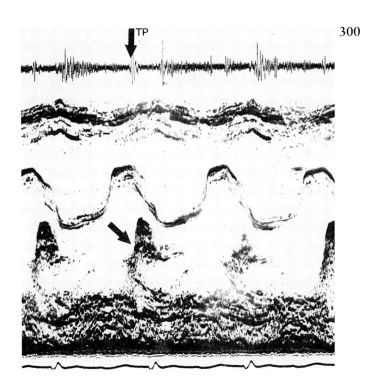

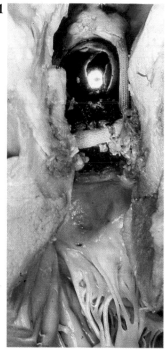

301

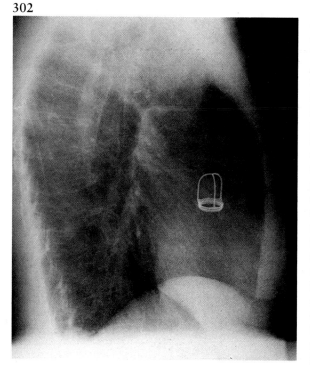

302

301–304 Mechanical valves produce typical heart sounds. An opened aortic root demonstrating a Starr–Edwards valve lying *in situ* is shown in **301** and can also be demonstrated on chest x-ray (**302**). An aortic Starr valve produces an ejection sound on opening and the closing click (CC) occurs within the second heart sound (**303**). In a mitral Starr valve, the opening click occurs early in diastole (**304**) and the closing click occurs within the first heart sound. Different mechanical valves produce a variety of auscultatory findings.

303

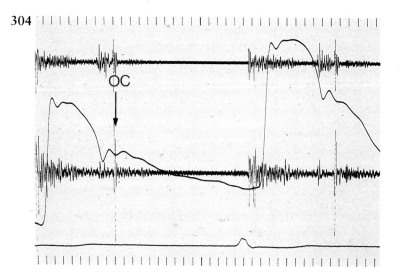

OC CC   APEX

304

OC

HEART MURMURS

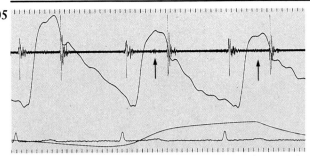

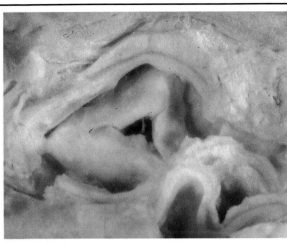

305 Quiet ejection systolic murmurs are frequently heard at the left sternal edge, particularly in children. They are usually short (arrowed) and there are no added sounds. The presence also of a normal second heart sound would suggest that the murmur is innocent.

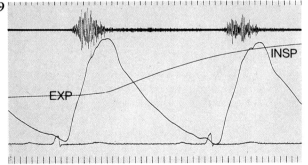

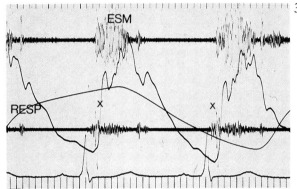

306–311 Ejection systolic murmurs may arise from the aortic valve or from subvalvular or supravalvular structures. **306** shows severe aortic stenosis due to rheumatic heart disease. The underlying aetiology in aortic stenosis may also be due to a bicuspid valve or degeneration. An ejection systolic murmur is heard in all forms of aortic stenosis and its length and intensity are related to the severity of the stenosis. A long ejection systolic murmur (**307**) peaks late in systole indicating the presence of severe aortic stenosis. In addition the aortic component of the second heart sound is absent. A bicuspid valve would be suspected if, in addition to the ejection systolic murmur, there is an early systolic click (X) (**308**). Characteristically the murmur is best heard in the aortic area with the patient sitting forward in expiration (**309**). Following an extrasystole, there will be potentiation of the murmur (**310**). In patients with aortic regurgitation a systolic murmur may be heard arising from the aortic valve even in the absence of any gradient across the valve due to the increased volume of blood crossing the valve (**311**).

310

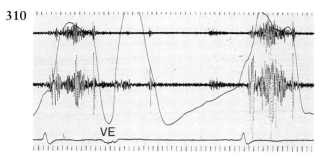

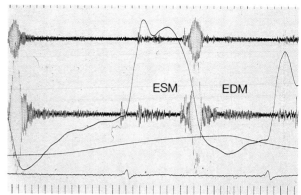

VE

ESM EDM

312

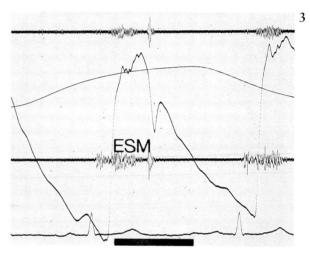

ESM

314

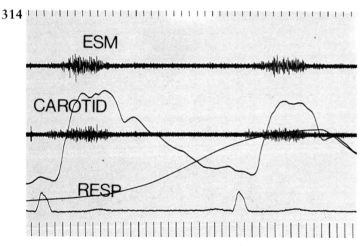

ESM

CAROTID

RESP

312–314 An ejection systolic murmur is also heard in subaortic stenosis. Subaortic stenosis is differentiated from valvular aortic stenosis by the absence of a systolic click and a normal second heart sound and normal pulses. An opened left ventricle in subaortic stenosis is shown in **312**. An ejection systolic murmur without added sounds and a normal aortic component to the second heart sound is present (**313**). Occasionally subaortic stenosis and valvular aortic stenosis can coexist in which case the signs of valvular aortic stenosis dominate the clinical findings (**314**).

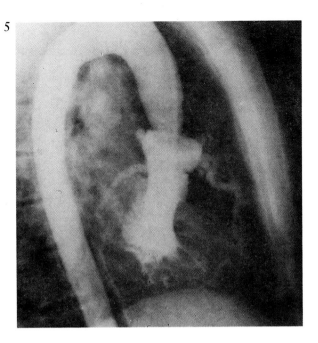

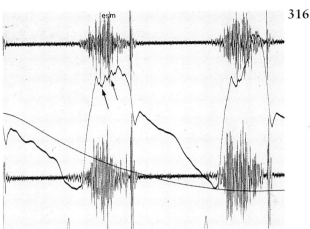

315 & 316 In supravalvular aortic stenosis there is an ejection systolic murmur and this needs to be differentiated from valvular and subvalvular aortic stenosis by the inequality of the carotid pulses. **315** shows a left ventricular angiogram (lateral projection) in which a supravalvular narrowing is present. There is a loud ejection systolic murmur with a coarse shatter (arrows) in the carotid pulse due to a thrill (**316**).

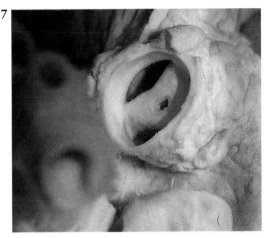

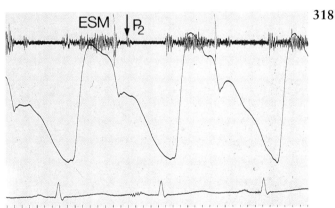

317–320 Systolic ejection murmurs may arise from the pulmonary valve. A stenosed pulmonary valve is shown in **317**. The severity of the pulmonary stenosis is broadly related to the intensity and duration of the systolic murmur and delay in pulmonary closure of the second heart sound. In mild pulmonary stenosis there will be a soft systolic murmur with only modest delay of pulmonary closure (**318**). With increasing severity, the intensity and length of the murmur increases and there is more obvious delay of pulmonary closure (**319**). With severe pulmonary stenosis the murmur is loud and pulmonary closure is not heard (**320**).

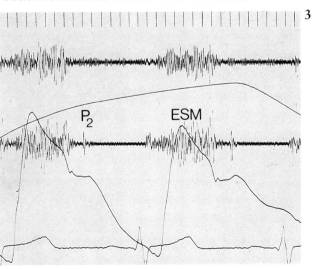

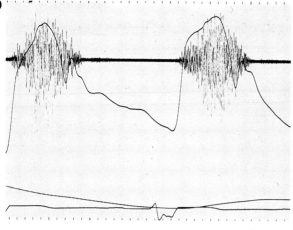

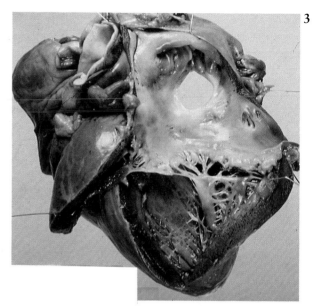

322

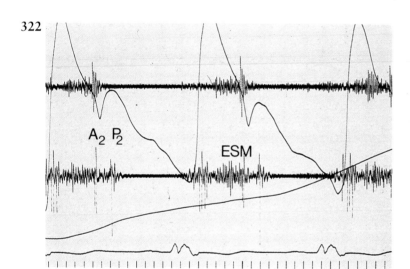

A_2 P_2

ESM

321 & 322 The murmur in atrial septal defect arises from increased flow across the normal pulmonary valve. An atrial septal defect viewed from the left side is shown in **321**. There is an ejection systolic murmur in the pulmonary area together with the classical findings in atrial septal defect of fixed splitting of the second heart sound (**322**).

323

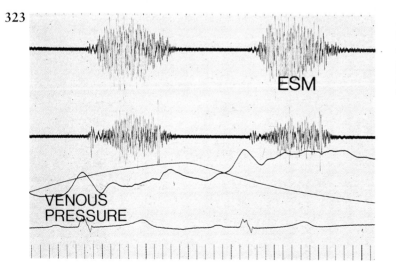

ESM

VENOUS
PRESSURE

323 Pulmonary stenosis may occur in the subpulmonary region where again a systolic ejection murmur will be produced. With a stenosis arising in the subpulmonary region the systolic click will not be heard.

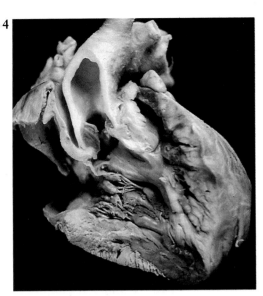

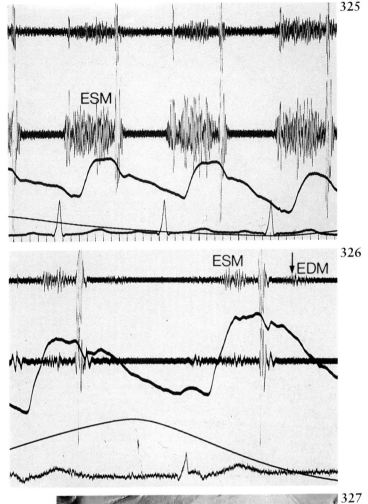

ESM

ESM ↓EDM

324–326 In Fallot's tetralogy pulmonary stenosis is both subvalvular and valvular. The pathology of Fallot's tetralogy is shown in **324**. The heart is cut in a right anterior oblique equivalent so that aortic override and the subaortic ventricular septal defect is seen as well as the pulmonary stenosis. An ejection systolic murmur arises from both the valve and subvalve apparatus (**325**); following repair a quiet residual murmur persists with delay of pulmonary closure (arrow) and a short early diastolic murmur of pulmonary regurgitation (**326**).

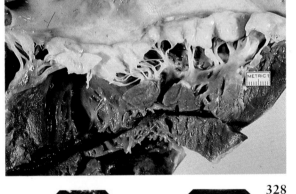

METRIC 1

327-330 Ejection systolic murmurs arising from the aortic and pulmonary valves must be distinguished from ejection systolic murmurs arising from the mitral valve. Occasionally an apical ejection systolic murmur may arise from the mitral valve, but in mitral valve prolapse, characteristically, the murmur is late systolic and preceded by a click. A redundant mitral valve with ruptured chordae is shown in **327**. Cross sectional echocardiography (**328**) will demonstrate prolapse (arrows) of both the anterior and posterior leaflets of the mitral valve in systole (left); in diastole (right) the mitral valve leaflets can be seen to be long and redundant. The murmur in mitral valve prolapse is characteristically late systolic (arrow), best heard at the apex and increased by squatting (**329**). These findings allow it to be differentiated from aortic murmurs, particularly bicuspid aortic valve. Simultaneous M-mode echocardiography and phonocardiography show that the murmur is generated by prolapse of the posterior leaflet of the mitral valve (arrows, **330**).

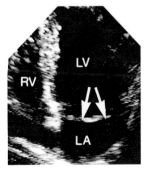

LV

RV

LA

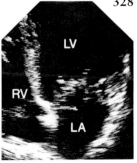

LV

RV

LA

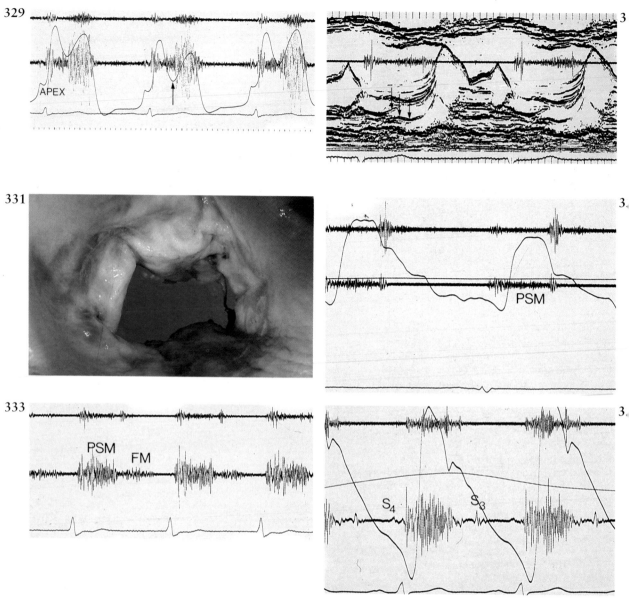

329

331

333 PSM FM

APEX

PSM

S₄ S₃

335

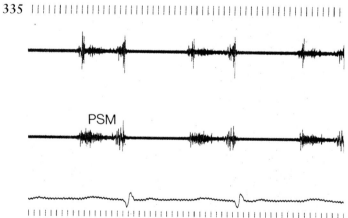

PSM

331–335 Pansystolic murmurs may arise from the mitral or tricuspid valve or alternatively from a ventricular septal defect. A non-rheumatic regurgitant mitral valve is shown in **331**. In mild mitral regurgitation a soft pansystolic murmur will usually be heard (**332**). Increasing severity of the mitral regurgitation is associated with an increased intensity of the pansystolic murmur and in addition there will be a flow murmur (**333**). In severe mitral regurgitation, in addition to a loud pansystolic murmur, third and fourth heart sounds will often be present (**334**) and following repair of the mitral valve, there may be a residual systolic murmur (**335**).

6

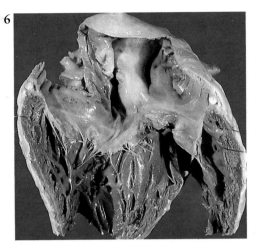

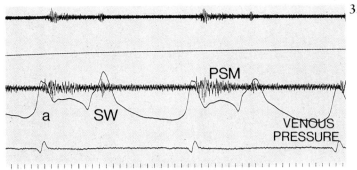

PSM

a   SW

VENOUS
PRESSURE

336 & 337 Tricuspid regurgitation is characteristically associated with a soft pansystolic murmur which increases on inspiration. In addition there will be a systolic wave in the venous pressure. A dilated tricuspid ring in dilated cardiomyopathy is shown in **336**. A pansystolic murmur and a small systolic wave on the jugular venous pressure can be seen (**337**).

338–340 Ventricular septal defect produces a loud pansystolic murmur and thrill at the left sternal edge. **338** shows a subaortic ventricular septal defect viewed from the left side. Characteristically, small ventricular septal defects are associated with a loud murmur (maladie de Roger); the second heart sound is normal and there is no diastolic murmur (**339**). A large ventricular septal defect will, in addition, have a diastolic flow murmur (arrow) with wide splitting of the second heart sound which moves with respiration (**340**).

338

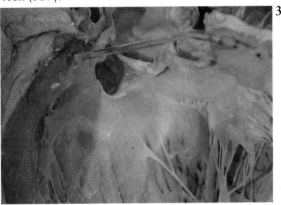

339

PSM

340

A_2P_2

RESP

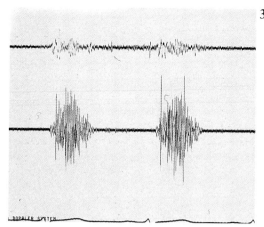

341 & 342 Ventricular septal defects may communicate between the left ventricle and right atrium (Gerbode defect). **341** shows a magnetic resonance image (transverse section) of a high ventricular septal defect between the left ventricle and right atrium (arrows). The pansystolic murmur is similar to that seen in ventricular septal defect communicating between the two ventricular cavities (**342**).

343

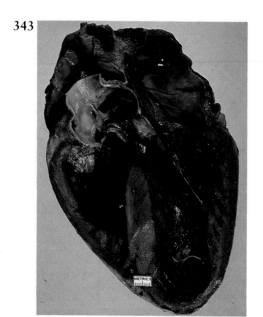

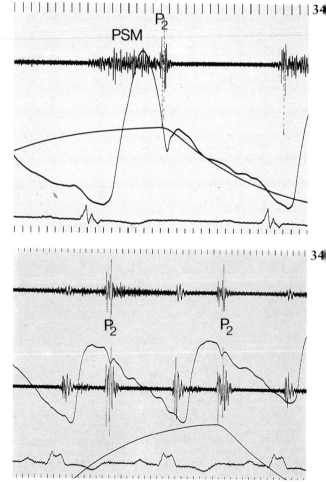

343–345 The development of pulmonary hypertension in ventricular septal defect (Eisenmenger's syndrome) will lead to accentuation of the pulmonary component of the second heart sound with progressive diminution of the systolic murmur. **343** shows a long axis section in the ventricular septal defect with pulmonary hypertension; the left and right vetricles are dilated. Moderate to severe pulmonary hypertension will result in a quiet pansystolic murmur with a loud pulmonary component of the second heart sound (**344**). When the right and left ventricular pressures are balanced, then the systolic murmur will be quiet, but the pulmonary component of the second heart sound will be loud (**345**).

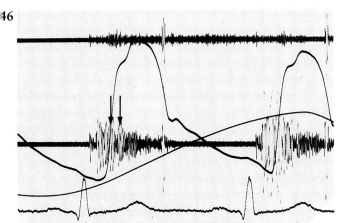

346 Ventricular septal defects may close spontaneously. This process may be identified by a change in the murmur from a pansystolic murmur to an early systolic murmur (arrows).

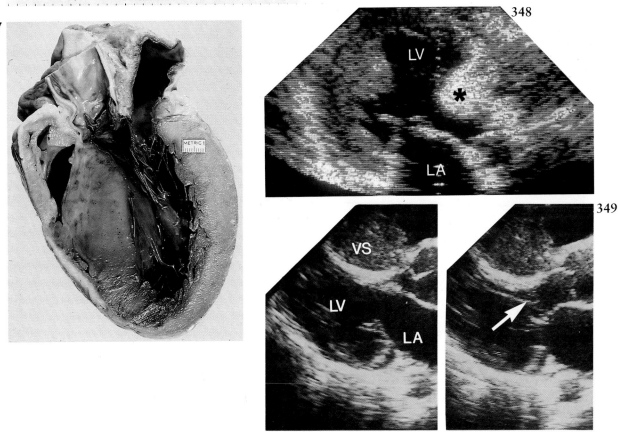

347–353 Murmurs of hypertrophic cardiomyopathy may arise from the subaortic region, in which case they will be ejection systolic, or may arise from mitral regurgitation, in which case they will be pansystolic; most have a mixture of both. **347** shows a long axis echo view of the left ventricle in which there is gross left ventricular hypertrophy, more marked in the septum than in the free wall. Septal hypertrophy can be best demonstrated using cross sectional echocardiography (colour encoded) in which the asymmetrical hypertrophy (✱) is localised to the subaortic septum and a large bulge of muscle is seen below the aortic valve (**348**). The subaortic obstruction is due to anterior motion of the mitral valve or subvalvular apparatus (arrow) obstructing left ventricular outflow (**349**). This is best demonstrated by simultaneous phonocardiography and echocardiography which show the timing of the systolic motion of the anterior leaflet of the mitral valve (arrows) to be similar to the onset of the systolic murmur (**350**). An ejection systolic murmur may arise from the left ventricular outflow tract (**351**); following an extrasystole there will be potentiation of the murmur (**352**). Characteristically the intensity of the murmur is increased by the Valsalva manoeuvre (**353**).

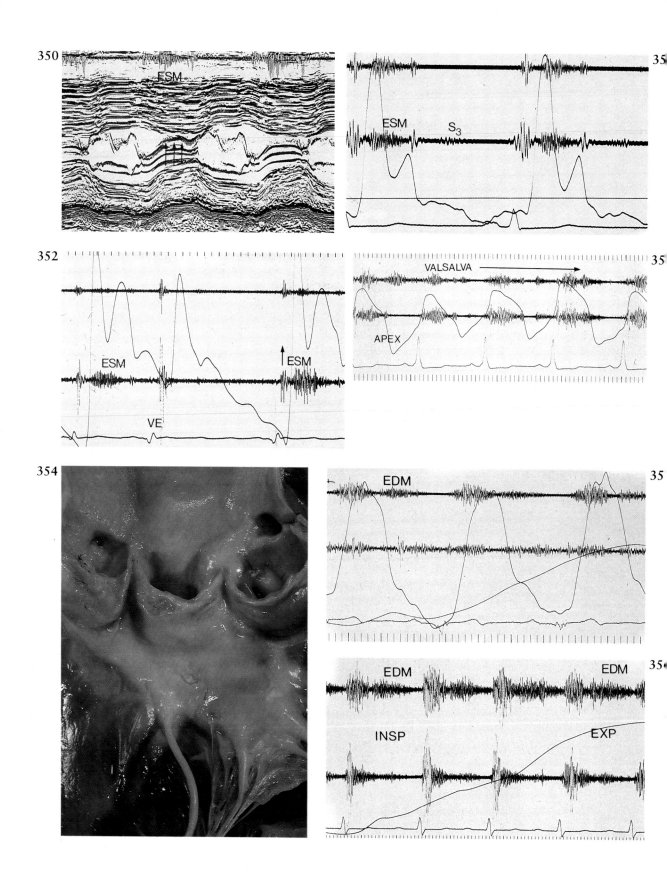

350 ESM

35 ESM S₃

352 ESM ESM VE

35 VALSALVA APEX

354

35 EDM

35 EDM EDM INSP EXP

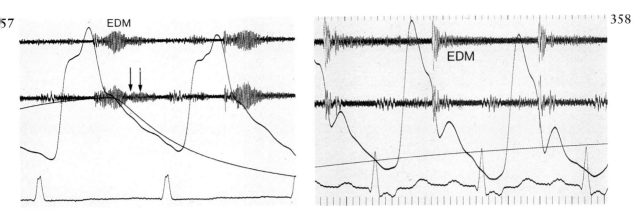

354–358 Characteristically, the murmur of aortic regurgitation is an early diastolic murmur which increases on expiration. **354** shows an aortic valve and adjacent anterior mitral valve leaflet in ankylosing spondylitis leading to aortic regurgitation. Dense adventitial scarring is present adjacent to the aortic valve commissures and extends below the base of the aortic valve producing a subvalvular ridge. The aortic cusps are shortened and diffusely thickened. In mild to moderate aortic regurgitation, the murmur is soft and decrescendo (**355**). The murmur is usually best heard in expiration with the patient sitting forward (**356**). In severe aortic regurgitation the murmur is louder, longer and may be crescendo–decrescendo in form; in addition there is a mid-diastolic murmur (arrows), termed an Austin Flint murmur, which occurs due to vibration of the mitral valve leaflets (**357**). The Austin Flint murmur must be differentiated from the murmur of mitral stenosis. An early diastolic murmur may also be heard when dilatation of the aorta occurs such as in Marfan's syndrome, pulmonary atresia (**358**) or hypertension.

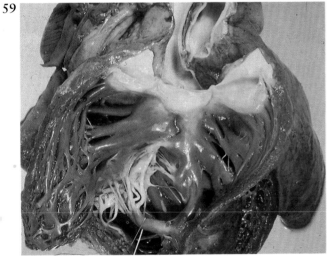

359–361 The early diastolic murmur of pulmonary regurgitation should be differentiated from that of aortic regurgitation. The character of the murmur is similar but is maximal on inspiration and is localised to the pulmonary area. Pulmonary regurgitation most frequently occurs in pulmonary hypertension, post-operative surgery for pulmonary stenosis and rarely may occur as a primary condition. **359** shows a dilated pulmonary valve and right ventricle in pulmonary hypertension due to mitral stenosis. Where pulmonary regurgitation occurs secondary to pulmonary hypertension (Graham Steell murmur) there will be an early diastolic murmur which increases on inspiration and follows a loud pulmonary closure sound (**360**). In contrast, following pulmonary valvotomy although the murmur is similar, the pulmonary closure sound is normal in intensity (**361**).

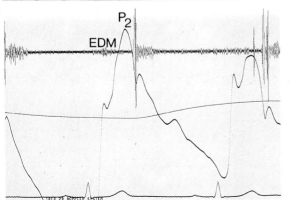

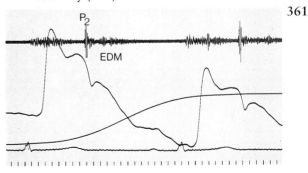

362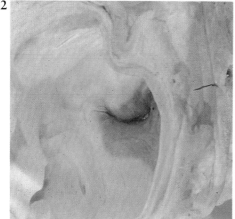

36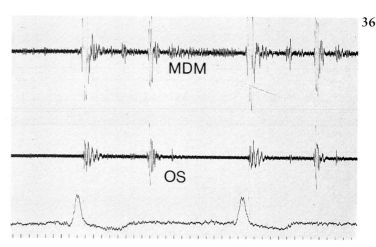

MDM

OS

364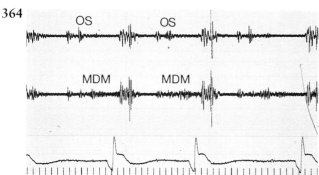

OS   OS

MDM   MDM

365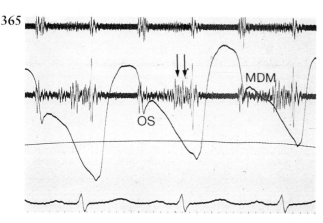

MDM

OS

366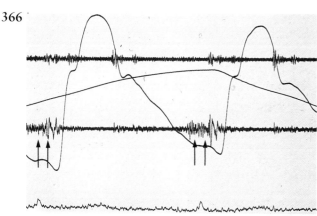

362–368 The murmur of mitral stenosis is characteristically a mid-diastolic rumble best heard at the apex. A stenosed rheumatic mitral valve is shown in **362**. In mild mitral stenosis a mid-diastolic rumble is best heard with the patient lying on the left side and may require exercise to accentuate it (**363**). With increasing severity of mitral stenosis the murmur becomes longer and louder starting earlier in diastole (**364**). If the patient is in sinus rhythm then a pre-systolic murmur may be heard (arrows) which follows an opening snap and a long mid-diastolic murmur (**365**). Occasionally in patients with mitral stenosis who remain in sinus rhythm the mid-diastolic murmur is soft, but the pre-systolic murmur (arrows) is loud and dominates the auscultatory features; this must be differentiated from a systolic murmur (**366**). It is important to differentiate mitral diastolic murmurs due to mitral stenosis from mid-diastolic flow murmurs (arrows) such as may occur in mitral regurgitation (**367**) and atrial septal defect (**368**), and also from the Austin Flint murmur.

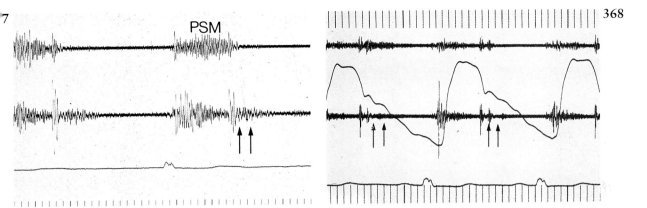

PSM

368

369–371 Tricuspid stenosis rarely occurs as an isolated condition and is usually associated with mitral stenosis. The murmur of tricuspid stenosis is similar to mitral stenosis and can be differentiated by the effects of respiration and its localisation. A stenosed rheumatic tricuspid valve viewed from the right atrium is shown in 369. Occasionally a tricuspid opening snap may be heard with a quiet mid-diastolic murmur maximal on inspiration at the right sternal edge (370). Tricuspid stenosis is best demonstrated using Doppler echocardiography which may show the presence of tricuspid stenosis and regurgitation (371).

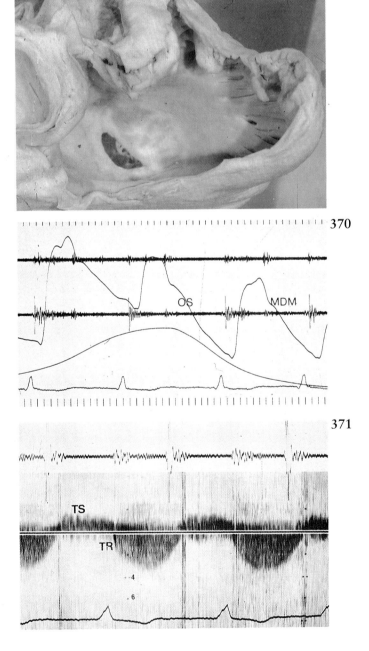

369

370

OS   MDM

371

TS

TR

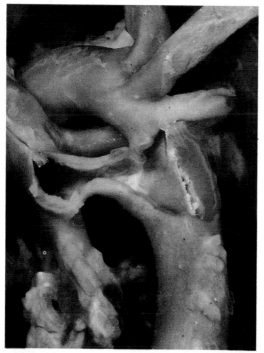

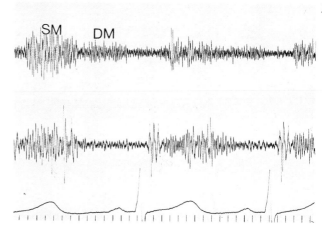

372 & 373 Continuous murmurs may occur in a number of conditions of which the commonest is probably patent ductus arteriosus. An opened pulmonary artery with a patent ductus arteriosus is shown in **372**. There is a continuous murmur best heard high on the left side of the chest and not affected by respiration (**373**).

374

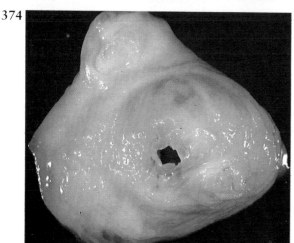

375

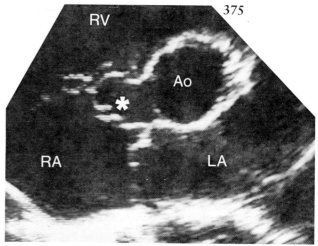

376

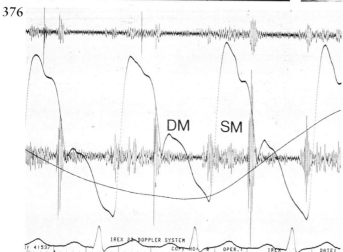

374–376 Other causes of continuous murmurs include ruptured sinus of Valsalva aneurysm (✱). **374** shows an excised sinus of Valsalva aneurysm with the site of rupture into the right ventricle. This is best shown in life by cross sectional echocardiography of the aortic root (**375**). The murmur is characteristically continuous though it may have a louder systolic component (**376**).

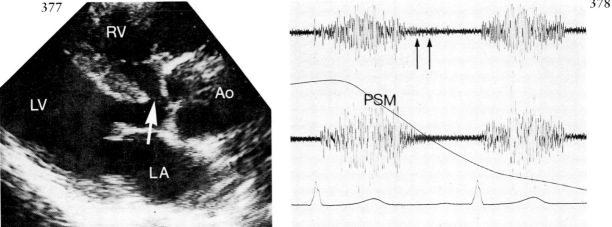

377 & 378 A subaortic ventricular septal defect may cause prolapse of the aortic valve leading to aortic regurgitation. The presence of the ventricular septal defect with aortic regurgitation will lead to a continuous murmur which must be differentiated from a patent ductus arteriosus. The ventricular septal defect can be identified using cross sectional echocardiography; the site of the ventricular septal defect is clearly evident as subaortic (arrow, 377). The murmur, although typically a continuous murmur, may be predominantly systolic from the ventricular septal defect and the intensity of the diastolic component (arrows) depends on the severity of aortic regurgitation (378).

379–382 Continuous murmurs may occur in arterial and less commonly coronary arteriovenous fistulae. **379** shows a right coronary fistula with a grossly dilated right coronary artery which communicates with the right ventricle. Large systemic collaterals may also give rise to continuous murmurs such as in coarctation of the aorta or pulmonary atresia. **380** shows an aortogram with a tight coarctation (arrow) and the presence of large systemic collaterals. Continuous murmurs in coarctation of the aorta are best heard over the back. **381** shows the large systemic collaterals that may occur in pulmonary atresia; in such circumstances, the murmur is localised to the area of the collaterals though these may be multiple. The continuous murmur from any cause has similar features and the underlying condition can only be differentiated by the associated clinical signs (**382**).

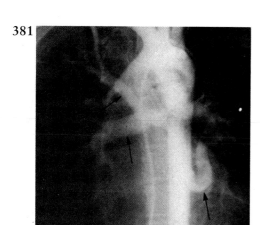

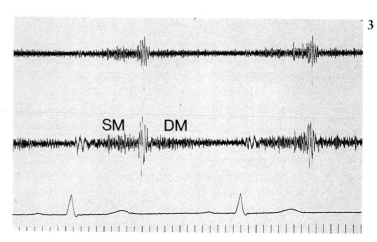

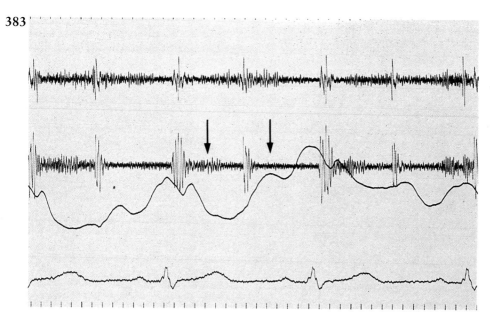

383 Continuous murmurs should be distinguished from a venous hum in children. A venous hum is a normal phenomena, it sounds like a continuous roar and is best heard over the right supraclavicular region with the patient sitting with the feet up. The venous hum will disappear with moderate pressure on the internal jugular vein. 383 shows the systolic and diastolic components of the venous hum (arrows) recorded from the right (above) and left (below) supra sternal areas.

GLOSSARY OF ABBREVIATIONS

A2	Aortic closure sound		MDM	Mid-diastolic murmur
AA	Aortic area		OC	Opening click
Ao	Aorta		OS	Opening snap
APEX	Apexcardiogram		P2	Pulmonary closure sound
CC	Closing click		PA	Pulmonary area
CP	Carotid pulse		PE	Pericardial effusion
CW	Continuous wave doppler		PSM	Pansystolic murmur
DM	Diastolic murmur		RA	Right atrium
EC	Ejection click		RESP	Respiration
EDM	Early diastolic murmur		RV	Right ventricle
ESM	Ejection systolic murmur		S1	First heart sound
EXP	Expiration		S2	Second heart sound
FM	Flow murmur		S3	Third heart sound
FP	Femoral pulse		S4	Fourth heart sound
INSP	Inspiration		SM	Systolic murmur
LA	Left atrium		SW	Systolic wave
LSE	Left sternal edge		T1	Tricuspid closure sound
LV	Left ventricle		TR	Tricuspid regurgitation
M1	Mitral closure sound		TS	Tricuspid stenosis
MA	Mitral area		VE	Ventricular extrasystole

INDEX

All figures refer to page numbers